Focus on IAM
(Identity and Access Management)

CSFs, metrics, checklists, best practices, and guidelines for defining IAM processes and implementing IAM solutions

Kiran Kumar Pabbathi

My eyes established a vision for my life,
After seeing the beauty of Lord Shri Krishna (with belief,
devotion and love).
My brain started working intelligently,
After understanding the morals of Lord Shri Krishna's
stories and his past times (with belief, devotion and
love).
My hands started writing good books,
After folding hands in front of Lord Shri Krishna (with
belief, devotion and love).
Oh Lord Krishna, what am I without your blessing,
Oh Lord Krishna, your blessing is the reason for my
breath, for good actions, for health, for prosperity, for
peace and everything that I possess.

Hare Hare Krishna, Krishna Krishna Hare Hare,
Hare Rama Hare Rama, Rama Rama Hare Hare,

Preface

Though IAM (Identity and access management) has become an eye-catcher for all CXOs, and niche skill set in all IT organizations (for the last 10 years) yet there are very few books on Identity and access management.
Among these very few books, none of them addresses topics like IAM process development, IAM product development, IAM consulting, etc. Hence, this book has been written to delineate a 'one stop solution' for IAM knowledge which includes information on IAM processes and products, best practices, guidelines, checklists, metrics and CSFs for all IT professionals (beginners, intermediates, and experts).

This book will help in understanding the key concepts of Identity and Access Management as a best practice, give an approach to design and develop IAM processes, and give an overview about developing IAM technical solutions. This book isn't the same run of the mill discussion about IAM philosophy and process details or just technical details; this book will be good for both process consultants and technologists.

This book can also be a reference guide and evaluation guide for customers who want to buy and evaluate the IAM solutions before investing thousands and millions of dollars on any IAM solution. It also provides good education and awareness information to all audiences (beginners, intermediates and experts) concerned with identity and access management. It helps beginners in understanding the basic terminology, key concepts, and functionality of identity and access management. It helps intermediates and experts by showcasing a sequenced approach for developing Identity and Access management processes and solutions.

This book can be divided into 4 parts as:
- Introduction to IAM
- IAM for Process Development
- IAM for Product Development
- IAM for Practitioners and Experts

Introduction to IAM will give insight on basic terminology, what is IAM, why we need IAM, challenges, benefits, and risks.

IAM for Process Development will provide a direction for developing IAM processes. This has been designed in an easily understandable way using 3 phases:
1. **Strategy for Identity and Access Management**
2. **Design for Identity and Access Management**
3. **Continuous Improvement for Identity and Access Management**

IAM for Product Development will give an overview on developing IAM products. This has been designed in an easily understandable way using 4 phases:

1. **Strategy for Identity and Access Management**
2. **Design for Identity and Access Management**
3. **Operations for Identity and Access Management**
4. **Continuous Improvement for Identity and Access Management**

These phases address all the key considerations to be made while developing identity and access management solutions.

IAM for Practitioners and Experts will discuss very rarely available knowledge on areas like IAM consulting, approach for implementing IAM products, new functionalities in IAM, evolving trends in IAM, technology in IAM, guidelines, best practices, checklists and many more interesting topics.

I wouldn't say that this is detailed and complete information, but definitely it gives a sufficient direction on how to develop identity and access management processes and solutions in a sequenced approach with all key elements.

All the guidelines, checklists, best practices are based on my observations, consulting experiences, and synthesis of knowledge; they do not represent any standard's documentation or best practice or any industry defined benchmarks.

Acknowledgements

If I have to start thanking people name by name,
I would first like to thank my mother Krishna Kumari Pabbathi for giving birth to me with all the organs and body in good condition,
I would like to thank my father Surya Prakash Pabbathi for teaching me the right morals and values. Also, I would like to thank him for placing me in one of the best schools which meant sacrificing his comforts and pleasures,
I would like to thank my grandfather Satyanarayana Pabbathi, who iterated that good books are the greatest friends, and exemplified his life for principles,
I would like to thank Balasaraswathi Penmetsa, for teaching Mathematics patiently in my 10th grade class, when I was poor at Mathematics, and when no professional teacher could teach me with patience,
I would like to thank my graduation friend Venkatesham Padigela who inspired me to become a topper in my graduation,
I would like to thank my friend Subba Rao for helping me and supporting me in many instances of my life,
I would like to thank my wife Divya for giving up her career and always bearing with me while showing great patience, calmness, and sweetness;
I would like to thank my first spiritual almamater - ISKCON and my first spiritual mentor Kalakanta Prabhu

8

for making me understand life and Lord Krishna (which is the best thing that ever happened in all my life)

I know that I am still missing numerous people who have taught, helped, and supported me numerous times in my life.
Hence, I would like to give my highest respect and surrender to **Supreme Lord Krishna** for arranging all these wonderful people in my life, and for giving me so many lessons, experiences and knowledge!!!

Special thanks to my Manager and CEO **Xiaogang, Wei** (Simon) who helped me in crediting most of my certifications, gave me an opportunity to work in his company, and gave me the idea to write this book.

Also my special thanks to my colleagues **Zengying, Tu** (Andrew)-(feiquan16@live.cn) and **Weihua, Zhao** (Wade)-(gswh111@163.com) who has helped me a lot in providing very valuable information to write this book.

Big thanks to Angel Berniz and ServiceManagers.Org for publishing another book.

About the author

Kiran Kumar Pabbathi has worked for various companies in the IT industry which gave him detailed insight into the IT industry. Currently, Kiran works as a Quality and Process manager in Shanghai Bizenit Information Technology, China.

Kiran had the privilege to work in different roles taking care of service desk operations, request fulfilment, incident management, SharePoint Administration, project management, ITIL consulting, ITAM consulting, and IAM consulting.

Kiran is a certified professional in ITIL® v3 Expert, PRINCE2 ® (Foundation and Practitioner), Six Sigma Green Belt, ISO/IEC20K – Foundation, TMAP – Foundation (Test Management Professional), Cloud Computing foundation, MCP in SharePoint 2003 Customizations, and MCTS in MS Project 2007.

His other authoring works include:
- "PDCA for ITIL – Metrics, CSFs and workflows for implementing ITIL/ ITSM practices" published by TSO, UK (ISBN 9780117082076) which details the procedure for implementing ITIL processes in an organization. This book provides direction for all

the 26 processes and 4 functions in a very easily understandable way.

- "Guidance for ITAM – Step by step implementation guide with workflows, metrics, best practices and checklists" published by Servicemanager's.org (ISBN 9780991320509) which details the guidance for planning, developing, checking and improving 11 ITAM processes with KPIs, best practices, workflows and checklists.

- "Charm of friendship" published in India (ISBN 9789382715924) which tells stories for children about friendship, how good friends can brighten up one's life and how bad friends can ruin one's life.

- "Guidance for EAM – Processes, Implementation steps, workflows, metrics, best practices and checklists" published by Servicemanager's.org (ISBN 9780991320516) which details the guidance for planning, developing and improving EAM processes with KPIs, best practices, workflows and checklists.

Why this book?

This book has been written to provide a direction for designing, implementing IAM processes and solutions, considering the experiences I have gained in my consulting career. It is going to deal with the niche, demanding and topics like:

- How does IAM help organizations, IT department, and end users?
- How to design IAM processes and solutions?
- Evaluation guide for IAM solutions.
- What is IAM consulting?
- Approach for implementing IAM solutions.
- What are the new trends in IAM.
- Maturity levels in IAM implementation.
- CSFs, best practices, and metrics.
- Checklists and Guidelines.

Table of contents

14

20

Table of Figures

Register This Book

Thank you very much for purchasing this book.

First of all, before you read ahead, please **register your book** here:

https://servicemanagers.org/iam-registration

As a **ServiceManagers.Org IAM Book Club** member, you will receive lots of benefits and support from our Book Club Forum:

https://servicemanagers.org/iam-book-club

Certification Program

This is the official book for taking the **ServiceManagers.Org Identity and Access Management Professional (IAMP)** program:
https://servicemanagers.org/iam-certification
This Career Program will improve your job opportunities and certify your skills gained from this book.

The Certification Exam is online, and once you sign up you can take it whenever you want (no deadline limits). Just sign up today for your exam, and start enjoying this book.

Frequently asked questions on IAM

What is the difference between Identity management, Identity governance, and Identity analytics?

Identity management is the discipline which focuses on the management of end-user identity lifecycles.

Identity governance is the discipline which focuses on setting direction, controls, defining roles and responsibilities for effective management of user identities and its respective access privileges.

Identity analytics is the discipline which focuses on the analysis of identities, its actions, and patterns to make intelligent decisions.

How much does it cost for implementing IAM products in an organization?

There are no such calculators to estimate the costs for implementing IAM products in an organization, as it's completely based on the requirements of the organization.

So it's absolutely unpredictable for estimating the costs of IAM products.

What comes first and what is more important, Security or Compliance?

Let's first understand the definitions:

Information Security: Practice which is designed to protect the CIA (Confidentiality, Integrity and

Availability) of information to manage the risks and provide better confidence to its stakeholders.

Compliance: Adherence to the international standards, laws, proprietary works, etc. in order to achieve the business goals.

In terms of priority, what is first and second: Yes, security is first, and then comes compliance.

In terms of importance, both are important: Imagine if you are 100% compliant with your standards and your security standards are just obsolete and doesn't address the right areas, so what is the fun in being compliant?

At the same time you have impeccable IS policies and procedures; and the teams are not compliant, there is no fun in having that extraordinary IS policies too.

Hence security and compliance are both important artifacts for a risk free business.

Examples of compliance regulations are: SOX, HIPAA, GLBA, COBIT, etc.

Are there any best practices defined for selecting IAM tools?

Please refer the section "Checklists for identity management product selection" and "Checklists for Access management products" in this book.

Is there any best practice for implementing IAM products?

Please refer the section "Approach for implementing IAM products" in this book.

Is there any simple use cases for newbie's to understand IAM tools?

Please refer the topics "Business logics" in the section IAM consulting which is very well detailed in this book.

Does IAM have any role in cloud computing?

IAM has great importance and would address many challenges of cloud computing; you can check the details in the section "IAM in cloud computing".

What software components are needed for IAM products deployment?

As a typical software deployment it also involves databases, web servers, middleware, etc. You can find detailed information which is addressed in the section "Technology in IAM".

What would be the best backend for IAM products? Is it LDAP or Database?

Again, it depends on your requirements; in my opinion it's better to use both of them.

It would be good to use LDAP for user objects and databases for transactional and audit data.

LDAP is good for storing user objects. Also it's event driven, lightweight, and provides better performance. But, it's not a good option for reporting and historical data like access rights, pattern analytics, system configuration and etc.

INTRODUCTION TO IDENTITY & ACCESS MANAGEMENT

Identity and Access Management

IAM is a security discipline that enables the right individuals to access the right resources at the right times for the right reasons. [Gartner Research]
IAM has evolved into mission critical discipline in IT for developing:
- ✓ trusted and reliable security
- ✓ effective governance
- ✓ improved stakeholders experience
- ✓ compliant business
- ✓ and reducing operational, administrative and maintenance costs

Note: Identity management and access management are not the same processes.

Basic Terminology in IAM

Access: Any information representing the privileges about the identity granting. Access rights for user identities can be categorized as create, read, update, delete, etc.

Access gate: A webgate that intercepts the requests of HTTP and non-HTTP resources.

Access management: Manages the access regulations to different assets and users by providing different types of controls. It enables one to tell very important information like who has access to what, who gave the access, when they got access, how they are accessing it, etc.

Biometric authentication: Authentication system where unique physical characteristics (finger prints, facial features, iris patterns in the eyes) of user are verified and validated.

Central user repository: Repository that stores and delivers identity information to other services, and also provides services to verify credentials submitted by clients.

Coherence servers: Servers responsible for maintaining and managing the cached data.

Common name (CN): Syntax defined in directories to store user names which is defined as user's first name [space] last name + GUID.

For example: "Van Jon – 9fv65653-g1ab-5678-8393-9e57ef7d1b39"

Cookies: Text files that are generated by websites and deployed on user's browser. It contains information like URL of the website which generated the cookies, duration of the cookie, login id and password, etc.

Credentials: A unique identifier used by the user to gain access on the information systems like PKI certificate, user password, biometric information, etc.

Data: Any raw facts or figures about IAM processes or solutions.

Demilitarized zone: Small network which acts as a neutral zone between a company's private network and the external public network. This neutral network adds an extra layer and enables stronger security for organization's LAN, without exposing the internal servers to outsiders.

De-provisioning: An activity which disables or deletes the user identity from the identity repository and removes the associated access privileges.

Digital certificate: Electronic digital attestation that

allows a user to share information securely over the internet using PKI (Public Key Infrastructure).

Directory server: Server that can add, change, delete, and store the users identity information like names, attributes, credentials, roles, groups and policies (Example: user name, email address, user id, password, etc.) in a tree like structure (normally in an alphabetical order) at a specific physical location.

Discretionary access control (DAC): Provisioning of access defined and configured by the data owner, who determines the access control based on his knowledge with respect to the requirements. This model is associated with capability systems; it uses ACL (Access Control List) to compare the identity of the subject.

Distinguished Name (DN): Name that uniquely identifies an entry in a LDAP directory. DN guides in locating, where the entry actually resides in a directory.
For example: "cn=Jan Bon – 9fv65653-g1ab-5678-8393-9e57ef7d1b39, ou=External, ou=People, dc=MS"

Domain: A logical group of objects (users, groups, devices) in an active directory with a unique name.

Dormant account: Identity that has been inactive (not being used) for very long period of time.

Entitlement management: Combination of processes or policies and technologies used to grant, resolve, revoke, and manage fine grained access entitlements to identities.

False acceptance rate (FAR): Percentage of the occurrences where an information system mistakes an impostor as a legitimate user and provides unauthorized access.

False rejection rate (FRR): Percentage of the occurrences where an information system mistakes a legitimate user for an impostor and prevents legitimate access.

Firewall: Network security system (combination of hardware and software) which controls and monitors the data flow between different networks.

Identity as a service (IDaaS): Another evolving service in cloud computing technology providing identity management as a service, which manages the user identities provisioning, de-provisioning, and controls their respective access privileges.

Identity provider (IdP) or Identity assertion provider: A provider (online service) that enables the users to assert their identity (which authenticates the users) using tokens. Identity providers create, maintain, and manage identity information for principals and provides principal authentication to other service providers within a federation, such as with web browser profiles.

Identity server: Server that manages information about users, groups, and objects stored in a directory server.

Information: Data that is well organized, processed, which follows a specific structure, and which is easy to understand.

Information security management system (ISMS): Is a management system based on business risk approach, which plans, analyzes, develops, implements and improves information security.

Identity: Any element or combination of elements that uniquely describes a person or a machine. It can be a user identity name, personal identification (ID) number, and etc.

Identity relationship analysis: An activity in IAM which analyses the user identity information (user identity information and devices) and its relationships considering the past, current and future user identities (internal users, partners, and customers).

IAM system: A system that contains IAM processes, procedures, repositories, applications to facilitate the identity creation, updating, control, and revocation.

IAM objects: Refers to all objects covered in identity and access management system. For example: Identity management server, Access management server, etc.

Identity management: Manages the lifecycle of digital identities for people, systems, and services.

Load balancer: Device which balances the requests between a client and two or more servers.

Logon credentials: Refers to the credentials used to identify a personnel and his/her access level to a specific information system.

Orphaned account: Identity that is not associated with any user or group, and has no information about who is using the account.

Protected resource: Any resource in IT infrastructure, which authenticates a user before being accessible (which is not freely accessible and available for all users).

Provisioning: Activity that creates identities, associates the identities with access privileges and adding them to an identity repository.

Proxy server: Server that acts as mediator between client and server or between two networks keeping the client machine's IP address anonymous for better security, also blocking malicious traffic and improving performance while accessing the same web pages.

Recertification: An activity of verifying, validating and updating the credentials with respective IAM system or identity repository.

Security token service (STS): Devices for authenticating and authorizing a user's identity.

Segregation of duties (SOD): Provision of clarity in roles and responsibilities, to perform a task with different roles/ individuals in identity and access management system.

Single sign on (SSO): A technical capability in IAM discipline that allows the users to sign in once, and gain access to the other protected resources within the same domain defined with same authentication level.

Strong authentication: A method which verifies user's basic login credentials (user id and password) and also verifies other form of identities like an electronic token or a biological identity of a user.

Virtual directory: Directory that provides a virtual view of different data sources and which aggregates data from different sources to create a single point of access.

Virtual host: Service provider who provides web services for the customers who do not want to buy and maintain their web servers.

Vision: Vision is a desired goal and intention, meant for long term sustainability of an organization.

Load balancer: Load balancer is a device which distributes the workload to different servers in a cluster, to increase capacity, improve performance and reliability of applications. Load balancers decrease the burden on servers, which manage and maintain the applications and databases.

Mandatory access control (MAC): Provisioning of access to users based on the criterion that is set as mandatory. MAC uses security labels and provides access based on clearance of subject. It uses a need–to–know system as its components.

Mission: Mission is the statement which defines the current status of an organization like 'what is the organization about', 'who are its stakeholders, 'what are its primary activities', etc.

Multi-domain SSO: Technical capability that allows the users to access protected web resources that are scattered across multiple domains with SSO service.

Goals: Goals are the broad objectives which are abstract and defined for a stipulated time period.

Objectives: Objectives are precise, specific, tangible and measurable accomplishments to be achieved by a business department, specific process, or a team.

Polices: Policies are management directives which significantly influence the processes and procedures.

Primary Authentication Server: An authentication server acts as a central server for all authentications in a multi domain environment.

Procedures: Procedures are sequence of actions to perform smaller tasks; it explains how to perform an activity, when to perform, what are the alternatives, etc.

Process: A defined sequence of activities that results in an outcome needed by the customers; it is performed with the help of people, products or applications, partners and various methods.

Proxy server: Web server which proxies requests to another web server.

Public Key Infrastructure: Information security software, hardware, processes and policies used in creating, using, distributing, storing, revoking and managing digital certificates.

Standards: Standards are rules and conventions that

37

help to implement policies and enforce required conventions.

Service: Provision of value to customers without the ownership on risks and internal costs to the customers.

Requirements: Needs of a customer presented as information in form of text or voice.

Representational State Transfer (REST): An architectural style and standard (stateless architecture that runs over HTTP) designed for accessing web-enabled applications, with a set of coordinated constraints applied to components, connectors, and data elements. REST supersedes the older standards such as WSDL, SOAP, etc.

Simple Cloud Identity Management (SCIM): A protocol designed for provisioning, administering, and managing user identities across cloud systems.

Token: Physical device that supports authentication of a user by generating a random unique code for accessing an information system.

Smart card: Identification card which contains an embedded integrated circuit which acts as a challenge response token. Smart cards are inserted into a compatible reader to get the user authenticated.

Web access management (WAM): Technology that offers integrated identity and access management for all web-based applications or resources. WAM can provide SSO and authorization services for heterogeneous web applications and portals without requiring thick client software.

Webgate: An application protection system (APS) that that intercepts web resource (HTTP) requests and redirects them to the access management server (for authentication and authorization); it also secures HTTP and SSL connections (It secures web servers by blocking attacks which pass through ordinary firewalls and packet filters).

Webpass: Web server plug-in that communicates between web server and identity management server.

What is Identity and Access Management?

A few years back, as per some ITSM best practices, Identity management was also called Access management or Rights management; and it was defined as a process for determining the procedures for granting authenticated and authorized users to services or resources in an IT infrastructure.

Today, identity management and access management is not considered as the same process; indeed they are two different processes, one managing the user identity lifecycle and the other managing access privileges with respect to user identities.

Of course, identity management and access management are two processes which are very closely associated with each other and hence they are collectively called "Identity and access management (IAM) processes."

Today, IAM is a practice that defines the processes, methods, and principles for user identity and access provisioning, controlling, and managing (in an organization, enterprise and federated enterprises). Identity & Access Management is a practice or process which consists of sub-processes (like account lifecycle management, access management and privileged access management, audit management, federated identity management, etc.), principles, specifications, metrics for complete and consolidated management of IT identity accounts and its entitlements. IAM processes takes inputs from other processes like information security management, capacity management, and availability management to develop effective processes and execute effective operations in IAM.

All IT applications access begins with user identity creation, granting of appropriate access, authentication, and authorization; all these sequence of activities are designed, controlled, and managed by the Identity & Access management processes.
IAM plays a very important role in every organization, irrespective of its size, revenue, and industry. IAM processes are very critical and foundational artifacts which can bring great IT benefits and business benefits; if it's not executed well, it can also lead to great risks like data loss/theft, data manipulation, etc. IAM occupies a very important role as it involves very crucial tasks on organizational user identities like creation, provision, reconciliation, administration, monitoring, maintenance, and de-provisioning. Also IAM is a very complex area which integrates different technologies, functionalities, and architectures across the organizations.

Key pillars for Identity & Access Management

Key pillars for Identity & Access management can be described by 3 important capabilities:

- Confidentiality
- Integrity
- Non repudiation

Confidentiality: Principle that protects the information and services by securing data from anonymous and unauthorized users, and by providing access privileges to only authorized users.

Integrity: Principle that provides assurance that information is not tampered by any other users.

Non-Repudiation: Principle that provides the assurance that a user cannot deny the work that has been altered by him.

4A's of Identity and Access Management

Identity and Access management enables confidentiality, integrity and non-repudiation through four important functions: **administration, authentication, authorization,** and **auditing**. It is also referred to as the 4A's of IAM.

- Administration:

  Administration functionality enables the IAM environment to administer all the digital identities in one place; it takes charge of activities like creation of accounts, modification to accounts, configuration of account passwords, assignment of entitlements, and modification of entitlements.

- Authentication:

Authentication functionality enables the IAM environment to identify and verify the IT user accounts, ensuring only defined user accounts can access the information systems. Authentication can be implemented using user id and password, using specific devices (like token keys, magnetic strips), and using biometric devices.

- Authorization:

Authorization functionality enables the IAM environment to determine what a user account/identity should be able to do in an information system. Authorization can be implemented through two approaches as coarse based authorization and fine-grained authorization.

Coarse based authorization defines an approach where user identities are provided with generic access to an information system.

Fine-grained authorization defines the approach where user identities are provided with generic access and also to very specific transactions which requires another authentication mechanism with respect to specific granular transactions.

- Auditing:

  Auditing functionality enables the IAM environment to meticulously log, track, and alert the administration team based on the actions performed by user identities. It also focuses on reviewing processes, standards, guidelines, procedures, and different technology related activities (authentication, authorization, user log in and log out, account creation, updating, and deletion, role creation, updating and deletion, password changes, account lockouts, synchronization events, and reconciliation events).

Why do we need Identity & Access Management?

Increasing demand on internet services and information systems (deployed onsite and in remote sites) forces service providers to constantly keep a meticulous watch on security, confidentiality, integrity, availability, and non-repudiation issues. ISM (Information Security Management) and IAM (Identity and Access management) are the processes which focus on strengthening security, confidentiality, integrity, availability, and non-repudiation issues.

IAM as a process or as technological element (in form of a granular task) is always a mandate for all kinds of IT services and for all organizations (IT service providers). Be it traditional IT systems like mainframes technology, client-server technology, or the latest cloud computing technology, IAM always existed right from the inception of IT service delivery.

With the increase in malpractices, hackers, snoopers, and eaves-droppers, IAM had a remarkable metamorphosis to strengthen the security of IT assets and services with the help of more mature processes and technologies. Identity & Access management prevents access fraud, information theft, non-compliance issues and enables the organizations with better security, confidentiality, integrity, and availability.

45

Identity & Access management (IAM) has become a vital necessity as a practice, process, product, and as an educational & awareness program for all organizations; poorly controlled Identity & Access Management process would incur high costs, loss of reputation, penalizations, non-compliance issues, etc.

Identity & Access Management for Organizations

Identity & Access Management for organizations will act as a framework which defines standardized processes, models, operational activities for the management of identity access requests, access provisioning, access control, access governance, access auditing and reporting. Benefits for organizations can be listed as:

1. Reduces the TCO (Total cost of ownership)
2. Single point of contact for complete information on all user identities and access on corresponding applications, resources and services.
3. Provides effective, improved security and timely access to their stakeholders (employees, contractors, partners, federated organizations, etc.) by reducing exposure to risks and increasing user productivity.

4. Develops compliance, solving issues that can occur at the time of audits which can lead to penalizations, and damage of reputation.

Identity & Access Management for IT

Identity & Access management for IT is a collection of activities like provisioning, reconciliation, authentication, authorization, de-provisioning, auditing and reporting. Identity & Access Management enables better guidance on the day-to-day management of users' accounts and identities across all IT systems. Benefits for an IT department are:

1. Provisions and supports secure data transmission and network access including VPN's, PKI's, etc.
2. Simplifies creation, updating, and deletion of IT accounts.
3. Simplifies routine and administrative tasks like password management and self-service.
4. Prevents unauthorized access to systems and data.
5. Provides detailed and accurate information on the IT resources 'Who has access to what?', 'When did they get access?', 'How did they get access?', 'Who provided access?', etc.
6. Provides end to end security for IT stakeholders.

47

7. Reduces burden on IT helpdesk by reducing the number of calls on identity issues like account creation, updating on account details, account lockout issues, password reset, etc.

Identity & Access Management for Users

Identity and access management for users provides many benefits, such as:
1. Reduces the time taken for new employees to get access to organizational resources.
2. Reduces the tedious efforts of users to remember numerous user IDs and passwords for various applications.
3. Enhances user's productivity and satisfaction by eliminating the waiting time on common issues like account lockout, updating personal information, etc.

Main goal of IAM is to initiate, capture, record, control and manage user identities and their related access permissions on organizational resources and assets. The ultimate goal of IAM is to provide the right access at the right time for the right people.

Identity and access management for organizations

A few years back, management of user identities and access privileges in an organization was a complex process which involved tedious tasks like creation of user identities (on time, with a specific standard), granting access privileges, monitoring the user identities and privileges, and deletion of the user identities (on time as per the standards). And any negligence on performing these activities caused numerous issues, employee frustration, loss of productivity, penalizations, and loss of reputation.

Let me give you a practical view of identity and access management tasks back in those days:

When an employee joins an organization

- An employee joins an organization.
- HR collects all the information, and updates it into the HR database.
- HR informs the respective manager of the employee.
- The employee's manager sends emails to different application and platform administrators to create user identities and provide respective user identities and

49

associated access privileges (with respect to the job role of the employee).

- Different administrators then create user identities and set temporary passwords for different applications.
- It used to take a week's time or so, and then employee used to get access to all the IS's and organizational resources.

This was the procedure for getting access to organizational resources which triggered issues like employee frustration, loss of productivity for organizations, and complexity in work.

Employee at work

- The employee had to remember numerous user identities and their respective passwords (the biggest nightmare is to remember them)
- If the employee forgets the password or gets the account locked, he has to call the service desk and get the password reset or unlock the account - which used to kill the employee's productivity.
- The employee had to login again and again whenever he needed access to the same IS.

These were the daily issues, employees faced at work.

50

When an employee decides to leave an organization

- The employee sends a resignation email to his manager.
- The manager informs the HR team.
- The manager informs the different application administrators to delete the account.
- Based on administrator's availability, the employee's user identities get deleted.

This was the procedure for deleting/disabling the user accounts in an IT environment which actually had many threats and vulnerabilities.

But today organizations are fortunate that identity and access management processes and tools have eliminated all these routine, complex activities and have automated many manual tasks eliminating manual errors, frequently occurring vulnerabilities, and threats. Let me give you a practical view of identity management processes and tools, now:

When an employee joins an organization

- An employee joins an organization.
- HR collects all the information and updates it into HR database in consultation with the employee's manager.
- Information in HR database gets reconciled to identity management tools.

- Identity management tool identifies the new user information and creates user identities for different applications.
- In a day's time, the employee gets access to all the IS and organizational resources.

When an employee decides to leave the organization
- The employee decides and sends resignation email to his manager.
- The employee's manager informs the HR team.
- The HR team sets a rule to disable/delete the user account in HR database with respect to the last working day of the employee.
- Then, the HR database reconciles the issue with identity management tools.
- The Identity management tools disable/delete the user accounts on the last working day of the employee.

Employee at work
- The employee has to remember only one user identity and password that will enable him to login to all applications.
- With the help of SSO, the employee only has to login once and can access many web resources without entering the password again and again.

- If the employee forgets his password or the account gets locked out, he can unlock his account/reset the password through IAM tools.
- With the help of identity federation, employees can also access third party companies/ partnering companies portals with the same user id and password.

Challenges in Identity and Access Management

While IAM can provide good value for an organization, it is also involved with many challenging tasks as mentioned below:

- Management of IT accounts for different stakeholders
  Organizations involve various stakeholders in the form of Permanent employees, Contractors, Intern employees, Customers, Suppliers, Partners, etc. Managing all stakeholders IT accounts with precise access privileges would require meticulous attention.

- Provisioning of IT accounts
  Provisioning IT accounts for various applications, after on-boarding, would be a challenging and important task. Delays in IT account provisioning, costs loss of money and reduces the productivity for an organization.

- Provisioning of IT accounts by different system administration teams in different places

Provisioning of IT accounts for information systems is done by different administration teams based in different countries, and multinational companies face many issues in provisioning IT accounts with unified policies and processes.

- Regular changes in IT accounts.
  Changes in IT accounts may be triggered for a variety of reasons such as:
  1. *Inaccurate and inappropriate creation of IT accounts which would lead to redundant work and confusion for administrators, with orphaned accounts and many more issues.*
  2. *Changes in roles and responsibilities.*
  3. *Changes in personal information like last name, contact number, etc.*

- Support and maintenance on low cost, low risk, and frequent issues
  Continuous efforts are required on support and maintenance of low cost, low risk, and frequent issues like account lockouts, forgotten passwords, account deactivation, and access related errors.

- De-provision of IT accounts
  De-provision of respective IT accounts for different applications, information systems and

55

organizational resources at the right time (when the employee leaves a team and joins another team, when the employee leaves the company) will prevent great risks for an organization.

- Security provision from all kinds of devices
  Security provision from all kinds of devices like computers, PDA's (personal digital assistants), smart phones, and tablets - requires explicit protocols and markup languages to communicate on operating systems and browsers of different devices.

- Synchronization issues
  Organizations store identities as data objects in different data repositories. As organizations can have hundreds of discrete identity repositories containing overlapping and conflicting data, synchronizing this information among multiple data repositories turns into a challenging task.

- Availability and capacity considerations
  Inefficient availability and capacity designs for IAM systems can be the greatest hazard for organizations, resulting in incidents.

- Providing robust security for IAM servers

56

Providing strong security for IAM servers with demilitarized zones, firewalls, proxy servers, web gates, etc. would be another challenge for an IT environment; any negligence on security can cause disasters.

- Scalability considerations
  IAM solutions would mostly accommodate more and more users (partners, employees, customers, suppliers, etc.) with respect to organizational size; therefore, scalability is a very vital aspect which has to be considered while implementing IAM.

- Data migration from legacy systems to new IAM system
  1. *Migration of the humungous data from legacy systems to the new IAM systems "as it is", without any corruption or data loss, would require meticulous attention.*
  2. *Migration of the data at the time of mergers and acquisitions from different AD domain controllers and directory servers would be another challenging task.*

- Balance on time, cost, and scope
  IAM projects take a very long time, involve complexity (as it involves integration with different

technologies), and need many skilled resources (as it would need human resources specialized in different technologies and applications).

Hence, companies meticulously plan the time duration of the project, analyze the requirements, and appoint the right resources with right skills.

Benefits of Identity & Access Management

Some of the key benefits of Identity & Access management can be described as:

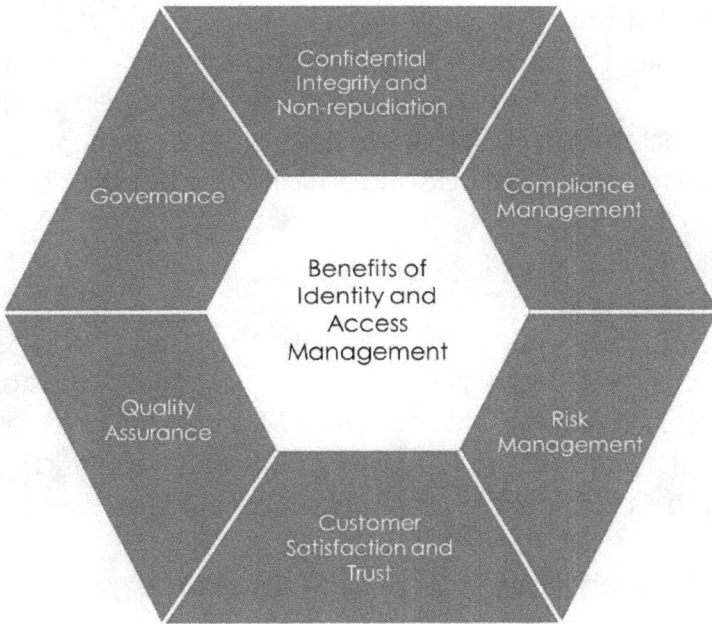

Fig 1: Benefits of Identity and Access Management

1. Improves confidentiality, integrity, and non-repudiation.
2. Improves compliance.

3. Improves customer confidence, trust, and satisfaction.
4. Improves governance and quality assurance.
5. Improves user satisfaction.
6. Reduces information security risks.

Improves confidentiality, integrity, and non-repudiation

Artifacts like authentication, authorization, access controls, SOD, PAM (Privileged Access Management), identity federation, and multi-factor authentication will provide effective confidentiality, integrity, and non-repudiation.

Improves compliance

Regulations like SOX, HIPAA, GLBA, Basel II have become a mandatory aspect for all multinational companies. Implementation of IAM can address all the threats with respect to information security and reduces the chance of non-compliance issues.

Improves governance and quality assurance

Defined roles and responsibilities, processes, procedures, templates and documentation inform the stakeholders about the unified approach on performing different types of long term and day to day operations.

Improves user satisfaction

Improves the user satisfaction through timely creation,

provision of IT accounts, and access to respective services and resources. Also new methods like SSO, OTP, finger print technology, etc. will reduce the chaos of working with numerous user identities and remembering various passwords.

Reduces information security risks
Information security risks are mitigated through well-defined policies, procedures, and different methods like authentication, authorization, audit, and control.

Improves customer confidence, trust, and satisfaction
Complete ownership and accountability on security of data, services, and systems with defined roles, processes, technological products, and regular audits which improve customers' confidence, trust, and satisfaction.

Risks for an organization without IAM

Risks that an organization can encounter without an appropriate Identity and Access Management System are:

1. Sabotage

   An act of deliberately destroying an organization's assets or data. IT industry surveys for the last decade mention that ex-employees were the leading sabotage culprits (in 37% of cases) who deliberately deleted or destroyed intellectual property and organizational assets.

   It also mentions that companies are experiencing many sabotage cases which have increased from 20% (2009) to 27% (2010).

2. Espionage

   Keeping a secret or furtive observation on another organization's information system or data repositories without the owner's permission.

   In IT industry surveys over the last decade, 41% of the IT administrators agreed that they used administrative passwords of different confidential systems to view most confidential and sensitive information. Furthermore, espionage cases from competitors and other vendors proved to be the biggest risk for many organizations.

3. Abuse of privileges
   Usage of access privileges either whimsically or out of curiosity (like viewing or downloading unnecessary or unintended information).
   IT industry surveys state that 50% of software developers are involved in abuse of privileges on different applications, databases, etc.

4. Data theft
   Stealing or copying an organization's intellectual property or confidential data and selling it to competitors or other vendors.
   There are numerous data theft cases in the banking industry, finance industry, and information technology industry (especially in the last decade), which resulted in organizations having to face heavy penalizations and great losses of reputation.

5. Data altering
   Modification of the data without owner's permissions to create confusion, discrepancies, and risks.

(Reference: InformationWeek Dark Reading - Internal Sabotage Security Risks Rising)

IT accounts

IT accounts are unique identifiers that uniquely represent a person/persons or machines. IT accounts can be categorized into two types as:

- Individual user accounts
- Public accounts

The individual user account enables individual users to log in to the information system and access resources. It is a unique identifier that represents an individual or user in the IT environment which is a collection of information (user id, password, dynamic code, etc.) that tells the IAM system about the access privileges, and allows the user to access an information system. It can be a user identity name, personal identification (ID) number, email address, etc.

User accounts can be categorized into two types as Internal and External.

Internal user accounts are the user accounts created for internal employees.

External user accounts are the user accounts created for external employees.

These internal and external user accounts can be further segregated based on the usage (where it is used in applications, databases, and mainframes) which can be mentioned as: windows accounts, database accounts, mainframe accounts, network devices accounts, directory accounts, middleware accounts, etc.

Attributes of the individual and external user accounts are:

Id: It is normally an integer or alphanumeric character, which is a unique number.

Url: It is normally a string, which is a unique string associated with a user account.

Secondary Id: It is normally an integer or alphanumeric character, which is linked to the Id and acts as an alternative Id.

Created on: It is normally the date in the format <DD/MM/YY> or <YY/MM/DD> or <MM/YY/DD>, when the account got created.

Disabled on: It is normally the date in the format <DD/MM/YY> or <YY/MM/DD> or <MM/YY/DD>, when the account got disabled.

Locked: It is normally a Boolean value, like true or false, which mentions the status of the user account whether if it is locked or not.

True depicting the status of the user account/identity as locked.

False depicting the status of the user account/identity as unlocked.

Enabled: It is normally a Boolean value, like true or false, which mentions the status of the user account whether if it is enabled or disabled.

True depicting the status of the user account/identity as enabled.

False depicting the status of the user account/identity

as disabled.

Public accounts are the user accounts which either represent a department or a role in IT environment; these accounts can govern and manage a collection of user accounts. Public accounts can be categorized into two types as group accounts and administrator accounts.

Group accounts are the IT accounts which represent a group/department or business unit of an organization. Group accounts are used to manage resources for multiple users. For example: hr_abc@abc.com, facilities_abc@abc.com, etc.

Administrator accounts are the IT accounts created for the administrators of various IT artifacts like servers, databases, applications, networks, etc.

For example: admin_hr@abc.com, admin_facilities@abc.com, etc.

Roles in Identity and Access Management
Role is a user account with specific set of access privileges that can manage and control a collection of user accounts. As IAM system manages numerous user identities/accounts, definition of roles can play a very important role in IAM system, making it easy for administration and maintenance tasks.

Let me explain it practically, imagine a company that has recruited a thousand employees in a month; after creating these identities, providing access privileges meticulously to different applications for every employee would take great effort, and would be vulnerable to many errors.

Hence, the feature called **Roles** is created which is just like another user account (with a collection of entitlements). Now, the employees are assigned to different roles by the IAM systems to reduce the complexity and vulnerabilities.

User identity lifecycle process

Employee Information Gathering → IT user accounts creation →Access provisioning → Account & Access monitoring →Account de-provisioning

Triggers for identity management would be:
- New user requests for identity creation
- HR team requests for creation of identities

Inputs:
- Employee submitted documents
- Manager provided details
- Information security policy

Employee Information Gathering

Employee information gathering is the initial activity which is performed by the human resource teams after an employee joins the organization. HR team collects the employee's information based on employee records, educational certificates, and other terms and conditions.

Mandatory information needed for employee information gathering are:

Employee full name

Display name

Nationality identity number/citizenship number

Employee's father name and mother name

Date of birth

Date of joining

Job position/ grade (i.e. A1, A2, A3)

Employee designation (Software Engineer, Software Quality Assurance Analyst, Development Lead, Quality Engineer, Quality Lead, Project Manager, Program Manager, Portfolio Manager, etc.)

Employment type (Contractual, Intern, Full-time)

After consolidating all the employee information, it is stored in the HRIS (Human Resource Information System) and a request for IT user account creation is sent to the respective IT team.

IT user accounts creation

IT user account creation process is triggered with reference to the request generated by the HR team. IT user accounts are created with respect to the information provided by HR team and the information stored in HRIS, in accordance with IS policies, procedures, guidelines, and standards.

IT user accounts can be created through three different options as

- Administrative account creation
- Automated account creation
- Self-service account creation

Administrative account creation is the task where an administrator takes the responsibility of creating the user accounts as per the information provided by the

HR team in synchronization with defined policies, procedures, guidelines, and standards.

Automated account creation is the task where a centralized tool creates the user accounts as per the defined workflows, policies, and standards.

Self-service account creation is the task where users create their accounts for specific tools, as per the guidelines and policies provided.

Mandatory information needed for IT user accounts creation are:

Employee full name

Employee number

Employee designation

Department name (IS, HR, Finance, etc.)

Department number

Manager's name

Manager's email address

Access provisioning

After the user accounts are created, they are assigned with appropriate roles and entitlements providing different levels of access privileges to different information systems. Access provisioning can be implemented by RBAC (Role Based Access Control), PBAC (Policy Based Access Control), and ABAC (Attribute Based Access Control).

Mandatory information needed for access provisioning are:

User account name

User account alias name

Email address

Role name (Administrator, Manager, etc.)

Policy name

Attribute name

Account creation date

Account expiration date

Account & Access monitoring

User account and access monitoring can be done either by automated tools, periodic checks, or consistent watch by an administration team. Account and access monitoring tracks, restricts, and logs all the actions performed by different users, giving detailed information for the management.

Mandatory information needed for account and access monitoring are:

User account name

User account alias name

Email address

Role name

Account creation date

Account expiration date

Last login date and time

Last login

Last password change

Last account lockout

Account De-provisioning

User account de-provisioning is the act of removing the access privileges and disabling the user's primary account, so that the user may not be able to use the primary/secondary accounts and access any information systems.

Mandatory information needed for account de-provisioning are:

User account name

User account alias name

Email address

Role name

Employee number

Manager's name and email address

Employee termination date

HR termination request number

Access management lifecycle process

Access requisition → Verification → Validate → Grant/ Deny → Document and Store

Triggers for access management would be:
- New user requests for access
- User request for changes in access rights
- HR team requests for addition or revocation of access

Inputs:
- Access request details
- Information security policy

Access requisition
Access requests can be raised through information systems or through filling a form. Access manager receives requests to provide new user access/ change user access/ revoke access privileges from HR team or Users.
The request details are logged in an information system, or manually in excel sheets.

Verification
User request will be verified with respect to requestors identity.

Validation

User request is validated if the request is legitimate and if the user role is supposed to have the respective access to the requested service.

Grant/ Deny

After the verification and validation of the user request, access manager grants the user request (if it satisfies the conditions as per the IS policy and role privileges).
If the user request is not a valid one or doesn't obey the IS policy or role privileges, the request will be rejected or denied.

Document and Save

Access manager documents the addition/ change/ revocation of access rights in an information system.

Manual procedures for identity and access management

Procedures for handling new user identity and access

- Request for creation of ID and specifies the list of servers
- Gets the approvals from manager
- Administrator receives the form
- Validates the details and checks whether if it's a new user
- Creates the username as per naming convention
- Assigns the password to username and sets the password expiry as per policy
- Grants the necessary privileges, as per the approval
- Verifies whether granted access is the same as required
- Sends the username and password to the user

Procedures for handling existing user identity and access

- Request for modification of ID and specifies the list of servers
- Gets the approvals from manager
- Administrator receives the form
- Validates the details and checks whether if it's

an existing user
- Modifies the username or user account details as per the policies
- Grants the necessary privileges, as per the approval
- Verifies whether granted access is the same as required
- Sends the username and password to the user

Primary stakeholders in IAM

Primary stakeholders and key contributors for IAM system would be:

- Human Resources team
- Information Security team
- Application Development team
- System Administration team
- Audit team
- Service Desk Support team

Human resources team

The HR team would be one of the primary stakeholders for IAM, as IAM work is initiated and closed with triggers generated from the human resources team.

The HR team consolidates all employees' information in the HR database and then the IAM team checks and refers that information to provision, monitor, and de-provision the users.

So, when the HR team works closely with the IAM team, the IAM team will be able to get complete details of employees and HR processes to build an effective IAM environment through directory services (Active Directory), identity management applications (OIM, SIM, etc.), access management applications (OAM, OPAM, etc.).

Information security team

Information security team is another key stakeholder for IAM and will work closely with the Information Security team; as all IAM products and operational activities are developed based on the Information Security processes, policies, and plans.

Consultation with the Information Security team while developing IAM products would bring great value focusing on CIA (confidentiality, integrity, and availability), adherence to business and IT needs, and reduce long term risks.

Application development team

The application development team is another key stakeholder for IAM and would work closely with IAM team for developing new functionalities in IAM products or for customizing the existing functionalities or features. Consultation with IAM team, at all stages of the IAM tool development/customization, would enable in developing effective, efficient, and defect free products.

System Administrators team

The system administration team is another key stakeholder for IAM and would work closely with IAM, as they perform all the daily operational activities in IAM systems (which includes IT applications,

79

databases, and directory servers).
Hence, system administrators should have a thorough understanding on the functionality and usage of IAM systems. And consultation with System administration team while developing the IAM products can bring great value and reduce many risks in the further stages.

Audit team

The audit team is another key stakeholder for IAM and would work closely with IAM. Consultation with Audit team can provide valuable inputs towards the development of IAM products, ensuring that the products provide complete assurance on achieving quality and compliance issues.
Checklists and best practices provided by the audit team can be incorporated into IAM tools and can prevent issues like non-compliances, risks, threats and vulnerabilities.

Service Desk Support team

The service desk is another key stakeholder for IAM as it will be responsible for managing routine and operational issues (e.g. password resets, account lockouts, access error messages, etc.). Hence, service desk teams should have a thorough understanding on the functionality and usage of the IAM systems.
Consultation with service desk teams while developing IAM systems would let management know about

routine issues concerning the service desk, enabling development of effective workflows and automated procedures.

Information Security Management

Information Security Management (ISM) is a process responsible for the development, implementation, monitoring, and compliance reporting of the organization's IT security policies which addresses confidentiality, integrity, and availability of information systems. The primary purpose of ISM is to develop, maintain, and improve confidentiality, integrity, and availability of organizational information systems.

ISM focuses on prevention of security risks/issues and will work closely with IT management and the associate communities across multiple work locations to bring the organization's information security risks under explicit management control.

Responsibilities of ISM

- Establish a global information security and risk management capability across the organization.
- Establish and enforce security standards and procedures including periodic, regular monitoring and reporting of compliance.
- Ensure that clear and timely business advice is provided to executive management on key information security and assurance issues.
- Advising IT management teams on information security issues and trends.

- Execution of audits and providing direction to remediate action items related to information security risks.
- Ownership of all IT security action items and working with appropriate internal and external stakeholders.
- Proactively conduct periodic security risk assessments and determine appropriate actions to address identified risks.
- Develop and deliver suitable information security awareness, training, and educational activities to associates, managers, and others as needed.
- Acting as the information security focal for the organization on a variety of operational security issues.
- Researching the latest industry security practices and technologies, as well as emerging threats and vulnerabilities.

[To develop more knowledge on ISM and ISMS (Information Security Management System), check the standards related to ISO/IEC27000 series]

IDENTITY & ACCESS MANAGEMENT SERVICE

Identity & Access Management Service

Identity and access management service is an approach for designing, developing, testing, implementing, and improving identity and access management processes and products for organizations.

Identity and access management service for process development is categorized into three stages as:
- ✓ Strategy for IAM process development
- ✓ Design for IAM process development
- ✓ Continuous improvement for IAM process development

Identity and access management service for product development is categorized into four stages as:
- ✓ Strategy for IAM product development
- ✓ Design for IAM product development
- ✓ Operations for IAM product development
- ✓ Continuous improvement for IAM product development

What are IT services?

IT Services can be represented in numerous forms, for example:

1. Internet available through an internet service provider
2. Software applications that are developed and delivered by a software development company

A service has to be well managed and equipped with defined roles and responsibilities by following specific quality standards and processes, so that the business can run without any breakdowns. To develop these services, it involves many internal costs, tasks, and risks. But, customers wouldn't consider or bother about the internal aspects like costs and risks in the internal development of a service offering; customers are only considered about the final outcome/result that is delivered by a service provider.

Any IT service development would require appropriate strategy, demand estimation, cost estimation, and risk analysis which lays the foundational tasks for the development of service.
Then, it would require appropriate design and development of service as per the requirements (in terms of functionality, availability, capacity, security, usability, etc.) and agreements; it would be followed by an evaluation of the service to check if it meets

agreed needs.

Further, it requires appropriate execution and deployment of the operational tasks to run the service. And finally, it will be completed through a planned improvement approach/initiatives which identifies flaws in the existing system, identifies improvements, and takes corrective actions at the appropriate time.

So any definition of IT service would require strategy definition, design and development, evaluation, operations, and improvement in a sequenced approach to meet customer's satisfaction.

What is Identity & Access Management Service (IAMS)?

Identity and Access Management Service is an approach that defines a complete lifecycle for the development of identity & access management processes and technological products. It involves defining and developing strategy, design architecture, operational activities, and continuous improvement initiatives.

Identity & Access Management Service is defined through four stages:

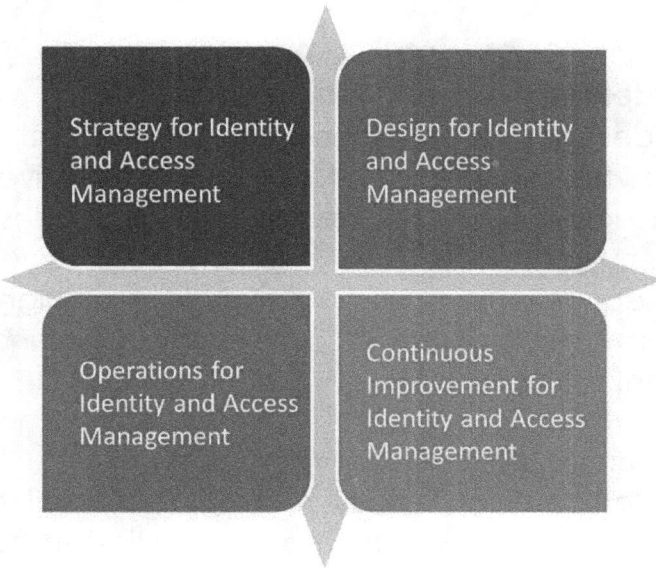

Strategy for Identity and Access Management	Design for Identity and Access Management
Operations for Identity and Access Management	Continuous Improvement for Identity and Access Management

Fig 2: Identity and Access Management Service

1. Strategy for Identity & Access Management
2. Design for Identity & Access Management
3. Operations for Identity & Access Management
4. Continuous Improvement for Identity & Access Management

Strategy for Identity & Access Management
Strategy for identity & access management defines the long term aspects to be considered for developing effective strategic assets. It involves providing strategic direction with vision, goals, innovation, and value creation for IAM processes & products.

Design for Identity & Access Management
Design for identity & access management defines the aspects to be considered for robust, effective, scalable, reliable, and secure identity & access management processes and solutions. It involves gathering requirements, defining high level design, low level requirements, architecture, and development of the solution.

Operations for Identity & Access Management
Operations for identity & access management define the operational activities (day to day activities) to be performed by operational teams like account

provisioning, de-provisioning, and access control and monitoring. It also defines the routine operational activities to be performed in identity & access management solutions.

Continuous improvement for Identity & Access Management

Continuous improvement for identity & access management defines the continuous improvement methods to improve identity & access management processes & solutions. It also defines metrics and critical success factors necessary for IAM processes, product development, and operations.

Who needs IAMS?

IAMS approach will provide great benefit to all categories of organizations, be it a small scale business (SSB), medium scale business (MSB), or large scale business (LSB).

All organizations would want to safeguard their data, protect their assets from any kind of risks and threats, and gain more customers' confidence, trust and satisfaction.

When an organization wants to manage user identities, access privileges, and develop an understanding among all stakeholders, it would need concrete IAM policies, processes, procedures and solutions/products.

When any organization has to develop and implement Identity & Access management solutions (irrespective of its size), it definitely relies on good processes, strategy, robust designs, and thorough knowledge of the products available. This is precisely mentioned in IAMS approach using the four stages: Strategy for Identity and Access Management, Design for Identity and Access Management, Operations for Identity and Access Management, and Continuous Improvement for Identity and Access Management.

IAMS approach can give good insight for consultants and management staff:

1. To develop their own Identity & Access management processes and technological products
2. To make effective decisions while purchasing an Identity & Access management product for their business
3. To customize an Identity & Access management product purchased from a vendor
4. To provide support on Identity & Access management operational activities

IAMS approach can also be helpful for students and other IT professionals who want to develop knowledge on Identity and Access management and Information Security.

IAM PROCESS DEVELOPMENT

IAM Process Development

IAM process development gives direction on developing effective, efficient IAM processes in a closed loop system. This approach is segregated into three phases as:
- ✓ Strategy Definition
- ✓ Design
- ✓ Continuous Improvement

Strategy Definition: Defines the roadmap for implementing IAM services in an organization. Also, it defines the long-term vision, objectives, and direction which lay the foundation for the process development and improvement initiatives.

Design: Defines the plans, processes, policies, and procedures, with respect to IAM, for enabling/aiding the IT staff in their daily operational activities.

Continuous Improvement: Defines an approach for improving the existing processes.

Strategy for IAM Process Development

Strategy for process development

Strategy for process development defines the long-term objectives and direction which lay the foundation for the process development and improvement.

Strategy for process development involves activities like:

1. Understanding the vision and mission of an organization
2. Understanding the goals of organization
3. Development of business case for processes
4. Definition of goals for processes and operations team
5. Identification of key stakeholders
6. Identification of key tasks and milestones
7. Estimation of costs
8. Estimating time duration for process development

9. Definition of process collaterals

10. Definition of processes
11. Definition of policies and standards

Strategy for IAM process development

Strategy for IAM process development can be defined through the below mentioned activities in a step by step approach:
1. Strategy definition
2. Costs and benefit analysis

Normally Process consultants, Process Managers, and Business Analysts with experience and knowledge in project management, ITIL, and Identity & access management would be considered as the best bet to perform these tasks.

Objectives

● Analyze and understand the business and IT requirements.

- To define strategic plans.
- Measure and evaluate the defined strategic assets.

Best Practices

- Strategy development as per organizational requirements and stakeholders requirements
- Development of strategy in consideration with innovation and value creation
- Evaluation of the strategic assets
- Shared vision and active stakeholders' involvement
- Effective risk and impact assessment methodologies

Strategy definition

Strategy definition for IAM processes will involve:
1. Definition of roles and responsibilities
2. Understanding the stakeholders and their requirements
3. Drafting the process blueprints
4. Analysis of the risks

Definition of roles and responsibilities

Definition of roles and responsibilities is the primary activity for developing strategy which would enable an organization to start off and carry out process development activities.

Primary roles and responsibilities in IAM process development are:
- Process manager
- Process developer
- Quality assurance analysts
- Technical writer

IAM Process Manager

- IAM process manager 'owns' the process end-to-end and is responsible for developing and maintaining processes and its relevant documentation.
- Preparing the process planning documents (quality plan, project plan including costs, resources and work breakdown structure, configuration management plan, etc.).
- Monitoring process development and progress.
- Act as a liaison between the IT organization, process development team, and customers.
- Act as a SME (Subject Matter Expert) for the process development team.
- Provides input to the ongoing Service Improvement Plan (SIP).

IAM Process Developers

- Documents and publicizes the process, policies, and standards.
- Defines the workflows, process manuals, Key Performance Indicators (KPIs), CSFs (Critical Success Factors) to evaluate the effectiveness and efficiency of the process.

Quality Assurance Analysts

- Perform verification and validation on the process collaterals
- Identify defects and discrepancies in process collaterals
- Suggest improvements and enhancements on the existing process

Technical writer

- Aligning content as per documentation standards
- Eliminating the grammatical and spelling errors in process collaterals
- Ensure the language is user friendly

Understand the stakeholders and their requirements

Most of process development works fail because of misunderstandings or inappropriate assumptions on requirements. Understanding the stakeholder's requirements is very much necessary for developing the processes. Stakeholders can be categorized into two types:

- Internal users
- External users

Internal users are the users who are part of the same

organization but are in different departments. Building identity & access management processes for this type of users would be flexible as there will be better communication, understanding of organizational policies, familiar infrastructure, etc.

External users are the users who come from different organizations seeking help on process development with specific requirements, dependencies, regulations, and constraints.

Understanding the stakeholder's requirements can be done with the help of tools like MoSCoW analysis and SIPOC analysis.

MoSCoW Analysis
MoSCoW stands for Must, Should, Could and Won't. It is a tool to identify "What is Must, What is Should, What is Could, and What is would (which would be in future)" for a service.

SIPOC Analysis
SIPOC is an acronym which stands for Suppliers, Inputs, Process, Outputs, and Customers.
SIPOC tool can also be used for analyzing the service offering to understand complete artifacts involved in a process (sequence of actions), major milestones, its boundaries, process inputs, process outputs, suppliers & customers.

SIPOC analysis helps in identifying:

- *Types of suppliers like internal suppliers and external suppliers*
- *Types of input sources and input variables*
- *Different processes (sequence of actions) involved*
- *Different outputs, outcomes, and output sinks*
- *Different types of customers like internal and external customers*

Drafting the process blueprints

Any organization's process offerings are primarily based on the three factors of time, cost, and scope. Organizations should draft blueprints of the process offerings with respect to time, scope, and cost specifications in consideration with different customer types and their requirements.

Drafting process blueprints involves:

1. Identifying requirements, constraints, and conditions.
2. Development of a business case for the IAM processes.
3. Identification of the resources needed (hardware, software, and people-ware).
4. Identification of key tasks and milestones.
5. Estimation of the time duration for completion of a process.

6. Definition of process deliverables, its format, and specifications.

Analysis of the risks

Risk analysis and mitigation is an important proactive and reactive approach which analyzes the risks, issues involved in the IAM process development and defines an approach how to mitigate them.

Identity & Access management processes are the means which acts as a baseline, and blueprint for the technological products, administration tasks, and operational tasks. Hence risk analysis and mitigation approach for IAM process development is very much necessary right from the initial stage.

General risks and issues for Identity & Access management process development are:

1. Misunderstanding on requirements
2. No customer involvement (regular reviews/ feedbacks) at the time of process development
3. Constant changes in IT infrastructure
4. Inappropriate documentation
5. Lack of knowledgeable human resources
6. Internal and external compliance issues
7. Inadequate funding from management

105

Costs and benefits analysis

Costs and Benefit analysis would be the final task in defining strategy for IAM process development.

Cost Analysis

This stage identifies the costs involved in IAM process development; costs are directly based on human resources, hardware resources, software (BPM tools), and other technology used in process development. Costs can be categorized into four types as:

1. Fixed costs
2. Variable costs
3. Direct costs
4. Indirect costs

Fixed Costs: Fixed costs are the costs which happen consistently and continuously for developing a process, and costs remain constant till a defined time period or project completion.
E.g.: Salaries for human resources.

Variable Costs: Variable costs are the costs which happen intermittently and which keep varying in the course of work completion.
E.g.: SaaS costs or bills.

Direct Costs: Direct costs are the costs which can be associated with a specific service development.
E.g.: Hardware and Software costs

Indirect Costs: Indirect costs are the costs which cannot be associated for a specific service development.
E.g.: Telephone charges occurred

An organization estimates all the above mentioned costs and quotes the final price for the development of IAM process.

Benefit Analysis is the analysis or estimation to evaluate and assess the benefits like profit margin, value creation, and brand reputation aspects for the service provider.
Benefits can be further categorized into two types as short term benefits and long term benefits. But with respect to IAM process development there would be no short term benefits, it would only have long term benefits as mentioned in the earlier section (Benefits of IAM).

Design for IAM Process

Design for IAM Process

Design for IAM process is the stage which collects detailed requirements, scope of processes, inputs, interfaces, triggers, outputs, outcomes, boundaries, dependencies, risks, and develops the process collaterals (encompassing process models, roles and responsibilities matrix, process guides, workflows, process posters, checklists, etc.).

Design for IAM process can be developed through the below mentioned tasks in a step by step approach:

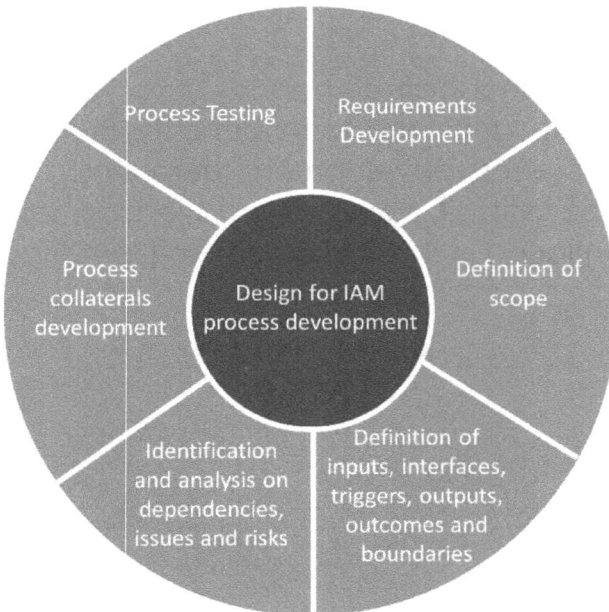

Process Testing

Requirements Development

Process collaterals development

Design for IAM process development

Definition of scope

Identification and analysis on dependencies, issues and risks

Definition of inputs, interfaces, triggers, outputs, outcomes and boundaries

Fig 3: Design for IAM process development

1. Requirements development
2. Scope development
3. Risk mitigation
4. Process development
5. Process testing

Normally, functional architects, business analysts, process consultants with good knowledge on identity & access management, ITSM, IAM technologies would be considered as the best bet to involve in this task.

Objectives
- To provide an overview and plan of the solution proposed to the customer
- To identify the risks and issues in the development of the solution
- To check the feasibility whether the solution can address and fix customer's requirements

Best Practices for Design
- Implement iterative approach for design activities
- Usage of best practices defined in ALM, TOGAF, etc.
- Documentation of learning from the previous experiences

- Consult the key stakeholders while making important decisions
- Usage of the right resources (with right skills) in the right activities

Scope Development

Development of scope is the primary and most important step for process development; the main objective of scope development is to define the boundaries for the process development work.

Scope development is the activity which comprises:
1. Scope planning
2. Scope definition
3. Scope verification

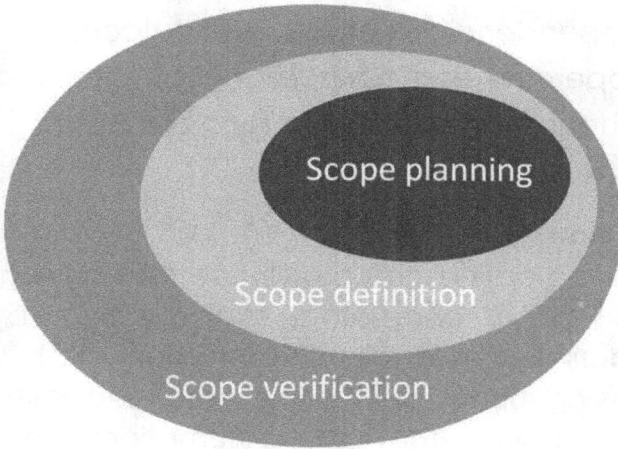

Scope planning

Scope definition

Scope verification

Scope development

Fig 4: Scope Development

Scope planning

Scope planning defines an overview of the process development work with project justification, project description, and its deliverables.

Scope definition

Scope definition defines the boundaries for process development work in terms of scoping and out of scope.

- In-scope or scoping defines different tasks and activities that are under the control of a process. It also involves identification of inputs, interfaces, triggers, dependencies, outputs, and outcomes.
- Out of scope defines the miscellaneous tasks and activities that are not controlled by a process.

Scope verification

Scope verification defines the procedure for verifying, validating, and acceptance of the scope defined by the stakeholders (sponsor, client, customer, etc.). It involves reviewing inputs, deliverables, and expected outcomes to ensure that all assumptions and estimations are meeting the customer's expectations.

Scope development ensures that all key stakeholders understand the scope of the process, project goals, and the statement of work as documented. It plays a very important role in estimation of the time period, costs, resources, and skills required for developing the process.

Human resources involved in scope definition should possess good understanding of the IAM process, ITSM domain knowledge, and project management knowledge.

Requirements Development

Requirements development is another foundational and important activity for the complete process development and improvement initiatives. Requirements development for IAM products involves:
1. Requirements gathering
2. Requirements analysis
3. Requirements specification
4. Requirements acceptance review
5. Requirements consolidation

Requirements for IAM process design can be categorized into five types as:
   a. Business requirements
   b. IT requirements
   c. Functional requirements
   d. User requirements
   e. Non-functional requirements

Business requirements
Business requirements represent the business or customer needs, business vision, mission, goals, and priorities.

IT requirements
IT requirements represent the IT needs, IT goals, and priorities supported by the problem areas or pain points in the IT.

Functional requirements
Functional requirements define the functionality of a software system which is depicted through inputs, calculations, outputs, and outcomes.

User requirements
User requirements represent the needs of different roles in IT operational departments and processes.

Non-functional requirements
Non-functional requirements describes the warranty related information for a specific proposed system like accessibility, compliance, scalability, security, stability, supportability, etc.

Approach for gathering and defining the requirements for IAM processes
- Elicit needs, expectations, and assumptions from stakeholders on the proposed IAM process.
- Understand constraints, conditions, and interfaces with respect to IAM process
- Understand operational scenarios in the IT organization
- Transform needs into requirements (business, IT, user, functional, non-functional, etc.)
- Obtain approval from the requirements

Key essentials for requirements

Key essentials for requirements can be described through completeness, correctness, and traceability.

Completeness
- All requirements should be written at an appropriate level of detail.
- Functional requirements should provide an adequate basis for design.
- All business and functional requirements should have a priority allocation.
- Requirements should include all of the customer needs.

Correctness
- Requirements should be free from typos, grammatical errors, etc.
- Requirements should be clear, concise with adequate diagrams, etc.
- Requirements shouldn't conflict with other requirements.

Traceability
- All requirements should be uniquely identified.
- All requirements should have the ability to link with each other.

Human resources involved in requirements development phase should have good understanding of requirements collection, analysis, and specification;

also, they should have good knowledge in IAM processes.

Risk Mitigation

Risk can be defined as any uncertain event that exposes a project to loss or damage of quality.

Risk mitigation is the continuous activity which brings awareness on risks and reduces the negative impact or loss or damage for the development of the process. Risk mitigation for IAM process development can be categorized into three areas as:

- Risk identification
- Risk analysis and prioritization
- Risk control

Risk identification

Risk identification in IAM process development should initially start with identification of constraints and assumptions to discover the risks for process development. Risk identification categorizes risks into two categories as general risks and specific risks that can occur in the process development. Generic risks are based on factors like time, cost, scope, human resources, skill sets, etc. Specific risks are based on process specific factors like functionality, integration with other processes, inputs from other processes, etc. *Risk identification can be done by methods like questionnaires, brainstorming sessions, and checklists.*

Risk analysis

Risk analysis involves understanding the risks, investigation of the root cause, and assessment of risk impact.

Risk analysis can be done by methods like 5Why analysis, Fish bone diagram, etc.

Risk categorization and prioritization

Risk categorization and prioritization involves:

Categorization of the risks which can be classified into areas like operational risks, financial risks, technical risks, resource risks, etc.

Prioritization of the risks can be classified as major risks, minor risks, and normal risks based on the nature, impact and likelihood of the occurrence.

Risk categorization can be done based on categories. Risk prioritization can be done by methods like pareto charts and histograms.

Risk control

Risk control involves implementation of changes (functionality changes, procedural change, policy change) to reduce or eliminate risks.

Risk control for IAM process development should be done only by avoiding all the uncertain possibilities. Transferring, accepting, and downplaying risks in IAM process development would only lead to humungous losses.

Risks in IAM process development

1. Misunderstanding and misinterpretation of customer needs during process development.
2. Inappropriate timeframes for process development.
3. Too much focus on technology issues rather than definition of process.
4. Inappropriate knowledge transfers about the process, procedures and policies.
5. Overhasty expectation of benefits.

Process Development

Organizations should first develop a stable, matured IAM processes, policies and procedures to manage their IT and other business processes. IAM process development is the activity which involves development of key deliverables like:

- Process goals
- Critical success factors, Metrics, and KPIs
- Process maps
- RACI matrix
- Process
- Process work instructions
- Process models
- Checklists and templates

Process goals

Process goals are the objectives defined for IAM processes; these goals should also ensure that they meet the business goals. Hence, goals setting should be discussed, agreed upon, reviewed, and signed off on by the key stakeholders.

One of the most famous methodologies for setting goals is SMART, which stands for Specific, Measurable, Achievable, Reliable, and Time-bound.

Critical success factors, Metrics, and KPIs

Critical success factors are the vital elements necessary for the success of a business. CSFs are the most important elements to be identified before developing IAM processes as the process development should happen based on the CSFs.

Metrics are measurements which can evaluate performance of IAM processes and operations through quantitative and qualitative definitions.

Key Performance Indicators are vital metrics necessary for an organization to meet its business goals; they represent the CSFs of an organization.

Process consultants should establish good Metrics, KPIs, and CSFs for an effective process. There is a famous quote *"You cannot improve, that you cannot measure; you cannot measure, that you cannot manage; you cannot manage, that you cannot define."*

Process Maps

Process maps are graphical representations of the sequence of the actions involved in IAM process development.

Process maps are used to track and document the sequence of actions involved in processes. Development of process maps helps the stakeholders in identifying the valued and non-valued steps

122

involved in a product delivery or service delivery. Process maps will also be of great help in communicating the information easily to other stakeholders and for training purposes. Process maps can be categorized into two types as:

- High-level process maps
- Low-level process maps.

High-level Process Map: High-level process map is a graphical representation of high level or abstract view of processes involved in a service or product design and delivery.

Low-level Process Map: Low-level process map is a graphical representation of all low-level or detailed information on tasks, milestones, decisions, dependencies, roles involved, inputs variables, input sources, output variables, output sources, and triggers for a process. Some of the common low-level process maps are Activity Diagrams or Value Stream diagrams, Flowchart diagrams, and Rendered process diagrams.

Responsibility Assignment Matrix

Responsibility assignment matrix defines the assignment of roles and responsibilities for a process, giving clarity and distinction to the roles and responsibilities using different types of matrixes like:

RASCI: RASCI stands for Responsible, Accountable, Support, Consulted, and Informed.

RACIVS: RACIVS stands for Responsible, Accountable, Consulted, Informed, Verified, and Signatory.

RACIO: RACIO stands for Responsible, Accountable, Consulted, Informed, and Omitted.

RACI: RACI stands for Responsible, Accountable, Consulted, and Informed.

Process

Process is defined by a collection and sequence of interrelated activities that yields a result or outcome required by a customer. These outcomes are achieved with the help of tools, roles, process goals, process maps, procedures, documentation, and metrics.

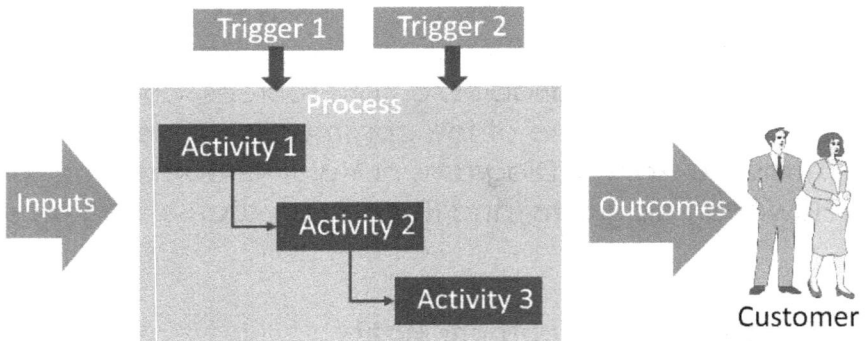

Fig 5: Overview of a process

Note: Process should have triggers, pre-requisites, inputs, throughputs, outputs, and outcomes to make the process effective, easy to understand and complete.

124

Process work instructions

Process work instructions define the detailed procedural instructions for different roles in a process for performing different tasks.

A good process should define detailed work instructions to make the audiences comfortable in understanding the process easily.

Checklists

Checklists are "To-do" action items in the form of questions which can judge the effectiveness and completion of a task or specific product or process.

Objectives of checklists:

- Reduce and eliminate failures and risks of a process
- Will act as a quick reference and saves time for the stakeholders
- Provides confidence and ensures the process is efficient and effective

Templates

Templates are the predefined layouts or patterns designed for some key documents, excel sheets, presentations, and any documentation deliverables.

Objectives of a template:

- Avoid reinventing the wheel and save time
- Avoid grammatical and spelling mistakes by composing all content
- Make the tiring documentation work easy
- Provide a defined common language while communicating

Process Testing

Process Testing is the last activity which reviews and evaluates the process designing collaterals like Goals, Metrics, Process Maps, Responsibility Assignment Matrix, Process, Process maps, Process Work Instructions, Checklists and Templates.

Testing on Process

Testing on a process involves verifying and validating the input sources, inputs variables, sequence of interrelated activities, outputs generated by activities, outcomes, process interfaces, information flow, and interrelationship with other processes. Also every process goal should be verified and validated to ensure they are correct, follow the best practices and standards, are SMART (Specific, Measurable, Achievable, Relevant, and Time-bound), and meet customer's requirements.

Testing on Metrics, KPIs and CSFs

Each and every metric, key performance indicator, and critical success factor should be verified and validated to ensure they are correct, can be measured, are aligned to the business and IT needs, follow the best practices and standards, and meet customer's requirements.

Testing on Responsibility Assignment Matrix

All roles and responsibilities should be should be verified and validated to ensure there is a designated role for every specific task, they are defined with respect to business needs and customer needs, and there is demarcation in responsibilities or segregation of duties.

Testing on Process work instructions

Each and every step in work instructions should be verified and validated to ensure there are guidelines or operating procedures with respect to every specific role, and that they give clarity and concise instructions without ambiguities.

Testing on Checklists and Templates

Each and every statement in checklists and templates should be verified and validated to ensure they are aligned with the best practices and standards, and that they address all the CSFs with respect to top level, middle level, and operational management.

Continuous Improvement

PDCA approach

Deming Cycle - PDCA (Plan, Do, Check, and Act) is a methodology for continuous improvement, and which is also called the PDCA (Plan, Do/ Develop, Check, Act) approach. PDCA approach is applied on IAM processes for effective control and improvement of IAM processes in order to make a balance on changing and updating requirements from various stakeholders.

Deming cycle is explained by the four phases Plan, Develop, Check, and Act.
Plan: This phase defines a series of activities to understand:

- What are the shortcomings, defects, and issues of the existing processes?
- What are the business operations which require definition of new processes?
- The importance of the improvement initiatives.
- How much time it would take to define and implement the improvement?
- What is the priority of the improvement (does the business really needs this initiative) and how

many of the users/ stakeholders would be benefited?
- What are the business benefits and user benefits of the proposed improvement?
- Does this improvement initiative adhere to any regulations, standards, etc.?
- What are the risks involved in this improvement?
- How much efforts does it require (in terms of human resources)?
- What are the different documentation deliverables which would be needed by stakeholders?
- Would this new improvement bring any new updates/changes in existing processes?

Develop: This phase defines a series of actions and activities that are needed to define and implement the improvement initiatives like:
- Identification of process owners or assignment of granular improvement initiatives to the respective process owners
- Definition of process review procedure, evaluating the effectiveness of an updated process
- Integrating the improvement initiatives with existing processes

Check: This phase defines the control activities to ensure that the improvements are developed as per the proposed plans, integrate well with existing processes, and meet the stakeholders' requirements. Activities involved in check phase are:

- Verification and validation in terms of technical review
- Getting the necessary approvals from management to publish the process
- Conduct internal audits

Act: This phase reviews the actions performed, identifies effective ways of doing things, and documents lessons learned. Typical activities involved in act phase are:

- Communicate process improvement goals and objectives
- Conducting trainings and awareness programs
- Conduct external audits
- Documentation of all the lessons learned

IAM processes & its relationships

Identity and access management processes, policies, and activities are a mandate for all IT systems; various IAM tasks (authentication, multi-factor authentication, single sign on service, coarse based authorization, fine grained authorization, provisioning of user entitlements, access certification, access governance, etc.) act as an interface for accessing IT systems (applications, databases, tools, directories, servers, etc.) and IT services. Without the interface of IAM technologies or tasks, IT systems and IT services would be unimaginable and would lead to disastrous fiascos.

IAM processes will have a very tight relationship with the other IT processes like Information security management (ISM) and Risk management. Also, it would be beneficial if IAM can integrate with other processes like change management and configuration management.

IAM and ISM

Identity and access management (IAM) has a very strong relationship with (ISM) information security management; IAM processes and tools development are primarily based on the policies, controls, and prototypes defined by ISM.

ISM classifies and assesses information, services, and assets based on sensitivity and priority. It also defines the security controls and policies, and develops ISMS (information security management system).

Hence, IAM takes many inputs and has a great relationship with ISM processes, policies, and procedures to develop secure IT systems.

IAM and Risk management

IAM has a very strong relationship with the risk management process of an organization. Based on risk assessments, identification, analysis, and control activities performed on organizational information systems, IAM processes and tools are developed and deployed in an organization.

Risk management identifies whether or not the organization has appropriate security controls for the IT and business systems, its users, and its data. It ensures to maintain if there are appropriate controls on confidentiality, integrity, and non-repudiation over the data.

IAM and Change management

Integrating IAM and Change management can also bring significant benefits for the IT organization.

As all types of changes (standard, normal, and emergency) are managed by change management process, it would also be a single point of contact for any changes on information security policies, identity policies, access policies, etc.

Hence integrating IAM and change management processes will enable the IT staff to:

- Monitor and track all the changes requested and implemented on information security concerns, user identity policies, etc.
- Follow standard procedures for changes on IAM products and processes.

IAM and Configuration management

Integrating IAM and configuration management can also bring significant benefits for the IT organization.

Configuration management is the heart of ITSM processes which consolidates all information about CI's, its attributes, and its relationships with other services.

Integrating IAM processes with configuration management will enable the IT staff to:

- Understand the number of IT services dependent on IAM processes and products.
- Understand the business services and IT services that are dependent on IAM processes and products.
- Understand the supporting IT services and configuration items in IAM products.

133

- Easily identify and diagnose the root cause of failures in IAM products.
- Estimate the business impact analysis of any IAM product's outage.

IAM PRODUCT DEVELOPMENT

IAM Product Development

IAM product development focuses on developing effective, efficient IAM products/ solutions for IT organizations. This is segregated into four phases as:
- ✓ Strategy for IAM product development
- ✓ Design for IAM product development
- ✓ Operations for IAM products
- ✓ Continuous Improvement

Strategy for IAM product development: Defines the vision and its plans for developing effective IAM products (via cutting edge capabilities and features with respect to the upcoming and futuristic needs of the customers) through a thorough analysis on the business and IT trends.

Design for IAM product development: Defines the architectures, functionalities, and features for the identity & access management products.

Operations for IAM products: Discusses the operational activities involved in maintaining the IAM products.

Continuous Improvement: Defines the improvement methods and approaches for improving IAM products.

Strategy for IAM Products Development

Strategy for application development

Strategy for application development defines the objectives, purpose, acceptance criteria and appropriate approach or development model for building applications understanding the demands from stakeholders.

Strategy for application development involves activities like:

1. Definition of the mission.
2. Creation of value and innovation in products or services development.
3. Definition of the goals and metrics.
4. Definition of the acceptance criteria in terms of functionality, number of defects, availability, performance, etc.
5. Definition of the policies for application development.

Strategy for IAM Product Development

Strategy for IAM product development can be defined through the below mentioned activities in a step by step approach:
1. Strategy analysis
2. Demand analysis
3. Risk analysis and mitigation
4. Costs and benefit analysis

Normally business analysts and process consultants with project management, and identity & access management knowledge would be considered as the best bet to perform these tasks.

Objectives
- Analyze and understand the business and stakeholders requirements.
- To capture and understand the demands of the stakeholders.
- To identify risks and develop mitigation methods.
- Definition of policies for application development.

Best Practices for Strategy
- Strategy development as per the organizational strategies and customer's requirements.

- Alignment of strategies as per the demands of the customer.
- Development of strategy in consideration with innovation and value creation
- Evaluation of the strategic assets.
- Shared vision and active stakeholders' involvement.
- Effective risk and impact assessment methodologies.
- Effective business and market analysis knowledge.

Strategy definition

Strategy definition for IAM product development involves:
1. Definition of roles
2. Definition of policies
3. Definition of the customer types
4. Definition of the patterns and priorities
5. Definition of strategy
6. Draft the service offerings

Definition of roles

Definition of roles and responsibilities is the primary activity for developing a vision and mission which would enable an organization to start off and carry out activities for the development of a service.

Definition of roles and responsibilities for different tasks and activities can be done using different matrixes like:

RASCI: RASCI stands for Responsible, Accountable, Support, Consulted, and Informed.

RACIVS: RACIVS stands for Responsible, Accountable, Consulted, Informed, Verified, and Signatory.

RACIO: RACIO stands for Responsible, Accountable, Consulted, Informed, and Omitted.

RACI: RACI stands for Responsible, Accountable, Consulted, and Informed.

Primary roles in IAM products are:
- Identity Manager
- Access Manager
- Identity Administrator
- Access Administrator
- IAM auditor
- Level 1 Analysts
- Level 2 Analysts

Identity Manager
- Identity manager owns the accountability of end to end identity management operations (operational activities like account creation, provisioning, de-provisioning, and deletion).
- Ensures the defined identity management process is followed in daily operational activities.

Access Manager
- Access manager owns the accountability of end to end access management operations (access granting, access review, access control, and access restriction).
- Ensures the defined access management process is followed in daily operational activities.

Identity and Access Administrator

- Performs administrative tasks like storage and archiving, backup, recovery, scheduled maintenance of the directories, and databases.
- Assists in investigating audit findings.
- Produces metrics and reports.
- Recommends improvements on identity and access management operations.
- Creates reports and submits it to Identity and Access Managers.

IAM Analysts

- Follows, analyzes, and enforces the IAM processes, policies, and procedures for the operational activities like account creation, provisioning, de-provisioning, deletion, access granting, access review, access control, and access restriction.
- Handles requests from end users and performs appropriate actions.

IAM Auditor

- Identifies the respective regulations necessary for the organization's industry, country, customer, etc.

- Ensures that the process, roles, responsibilities and documentation are regularly reviewed and audited.
- Assesses the current compliance baseline by analyzing the organization's risk and compliance policy, determining how it is aligned with industry best practices.
- Performs a gap analysis of IAM processes and reviews actual business performance against potential performance.
- Recommends the organization to implement IAM controls where needed and compares these to industry standards and best practices, such as the International Organization for Standardization's 27001 Standard.
- Perform regular audits.
- Conducts training and awareness programs to ensure all relevant staff has the required knowledge to perform their roles respectively.

Definition of policies

Policy definition involves defining rules and expectations, documenting them, bringing awareness about policies, monitoring and adherence to the defined policies.

Definition of policies would enable streamlining of all tasks and activities performed by different human

143

resources involved in IAM product development.

Definition of policies for IAM product development would bring many other advantages like:

- Consistent quality assurance and controls to the complete product development lifecycle.
- Protection of IS resources and capabilities without exposing them to any risks.
- Also helps in adherence to compliance at the time of audits.

Definition of customer types

Understanding the customers is very much necessary before developing products.

Customers can be categorized into two types:

- Internal customers
- External customers

Internal customers are the customers who are part of the same organization but in different departments. Building identity & access management processes or solutions for this type of customer would be more flexible as there will be better communication, understanding, understanding of the organizational policies, etc.

External customers are customers who come from different organizations to provide business and who need specific services delivered. External customers can be classified into three types:

- SSB (Small Scale Business) Organizations

144

- MSB (Medium Scale Business) Organizations
- LSB (Large Scale Business) Organizations

In this phase organizations should decide which customer would require what services - which is determined based on the vision and mission of the organization.

Definition of patterns and priorities

Patterns and priorities identify the technology, functions, business trends, patterns, and priorities which would enable the organization to understand what is needed by the customers, what is offered by the competitors, and what can bring innovation and value to its services.

Examples for patterns and priorities with respect to IAM solutions are:

- Evolution of new cloud service called - IAM as a service.
- Evolution of new concept called IRM (Identity Relationship Management).
- Evolution of new concept called PIM (Privileged Identity Management).

Definition of strategy

Definition of strategy for IAM products should be primarily be based on:

145

- Organizational strategy (overall direction of the organization)
- Business strategy (department or divisions goals and objectives)
- Functional strategy (focused on operational activities)

These strategies can be defined by adopting well recognized strategy development tools and methods like Porter's five force analysis, Value chain analysis, and finally SWOT analysis to evaluate the defined strategy.

Porter's five force analysis
Porter's five force analysis is based on five forces which can be summed up as: Supplier's power, Threat of new entrants, Threat of substitutes, Buyer's power, and Intensity of rivalry.

Value chain analysis
Value chain analysis is the analysis and understanding on the chain of activities (identifying the primary and secondary activities) that develop a product or service for an organization.

SWOT analysis
SWOT analysis is an improvement methodology to identify the strengths, weakness, opportunities, and threats for the proposed services or products in an

organization.

For example: SWOT analysis diagram for an organization

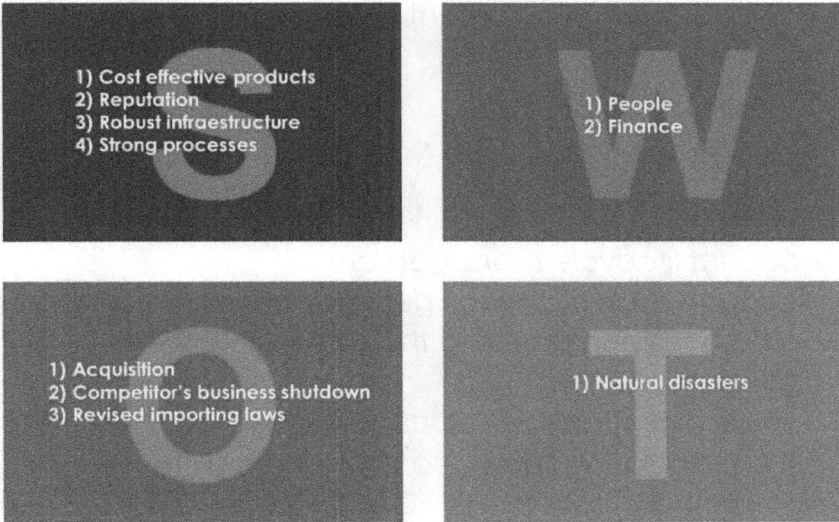

Fig 6: SWOT Analysis

Draft the service offerings

Any organization's service offerings are primarily based on the three factors: Time, Cost and Scope. Organizations should draft blueprints of service offerings with respect to the time, scope, and cost specifications in consideration with different customer types and their requirements. It includes estimation of the time duration, human resources needed, skill sets

147

required, and the costs involved.

Service offerings on IAM products can be divided into different areas as:
1. Account lifecycle management
2. Access management and Privileged Access Management
3. Audit management
4. Federated Identity & Access Management

Account lifecycle management
Account lifecycle management defines a standard procedure for managing the end to end lifecycle of IT accounts.
IT account lifecycle starts from account creation, proceeds to account configuration with necessary roles and privileges, continues with account maintenance, and finally finishes with account deletion.

Access Management and Privileged Access Management (PAM)
Access management defines the procedures for providing access using authentication and authorization methods on applications, databases, websites, computers, etc.
PAM can be referred to as an internal activity which is a part of Access Management. It manages the privileged accounts which can access very confidential and sensitive data in an information

system.

Audit Management
Audit management defines the procedures for tracking, verifying, and validating the IT accounts and access information at regular intervals to ensure there is an accurate snapshot on identity & access management system.

Federated Identity & Access Management
Federated Identity & Access management defines the procedures that enable trusted relationships between different domains so that users can authenticate to their own domain and access the applications hosted in other domains.

Identity & Access management service offerings (in form of process/ applications) will be based on the above mentioned sub-processes and specific requirements from the customers.

Demand analysis

Demand analysis gives valuable information to an organization about the business and the markets they plan to pursue. It is the area of predictive analysis for understanding products demand with respect to different consumers and predicting the future of a product. This understanding is harnessed and used to forecast the products demand. Knowledge on demand fluctuation enables the service provider to produce and offer the right services in the right quality and at the right time. Demand estimation should be considered with the great importance before investing any organizational resources on any product development.

The real purpose of demand analysis is to find the product's/solution's potential demand, so that managers can make accurate decisions about pricing, business growth, and market potential.

Demand analysis can be performed by using Qualitative and Quantitative methods.

Qualitative methods can be described as expert opinions, questionnaires, customer surveys, brainstorming, delphi technique, intentions survey, conjoint analysis, etc.

Quantitative methods can be described as data mining on the historical data, extrapolation (estimating the value and the demand of a service based on its dependencies), time series forecasting (predicting product's demand based on historic data), etc.

The objective of demand analysis is to:
1. Understand the number of SSBs requiring a specific product.
2. Understand the number of MSBs requiring a specific product.
3. Understand the number of LSBs requiring a specific product.
4. Understand the willingness of the customer to spend money without constraints.
5. Understand the complexity in technology/complexity in business.
6. Understand the innovation and value creation from developed products.
7. Analyze the other competitors' services and their pros and cons.
8. Understand the acceptance of internal stakeholders in the organization.
9. Determine the pricing for services.

Risk analysis and mitigation

Risk analysis and mitigation is an important proactive approach which identifies, analyzes, and defines an approach to counteract risks and issues involved in product development.

Identity & access management products are the means which unify various application users through a single streamlined channel (As organizations use different applications which are built on different technologies and platforms to fulfill their business and functional requirements).
Deploying identity & access management solution in infrastructure using different technologies and platforms could bring many issues and risks for an organization.
Hence, organizations should identify all technical and functional risks in product development, product sales, product support, product maintenance, etc.

General risks for identity & access management product development are:
1. Lack of knowledgeable human resources
   As IAM products are new in the IT market, human resources with knowledge on IAM processes and IAM technologies are difficult.

152

2. Adequate funding from management
    IAM products integrations with different applications involves huge costs; most of the companies give up on complete integration and instead follow manual work.

3. Improper/vague/unfeasible process definition
    IAM processes act as a baseline for product development (in terms of functionality); improper or vague or unfeasible processes would lead to inappropriate products.

4. Ambiguity in IS policies and procedures
    Confusion, misunderstanding, and misinterpretation of IS policies and procedures can lead to major failures.

5. Code changes/customization to applications, databases, and directories
    While integrating different applications, directories, and databases to IAM solutions, IAM consultants should ensure that they are not making major code changes impacting the functionality of other applications.

6. Usage of 3rd party tools

Usage of too many 3rd party tools for integrating IAM products increases more complexity and costs.

7. Scalability for future needs
    Improper planning of hardware and software may lead to risks like degradation of performance or disruption of service.

8. Integration with other applications
    Integration of different applications, databases, and directories (built on different technologies), and connecting them using different connectors and web services with IAM products would make maintenance issues more complex.

9. Assumptions on firewalls, proxy servers, and load balancers
    Integrating firewalls, proxy servers and load balancers with IAM tools(just as per the OEM guidance) might expose the IAM environment to some risks; hence, there should be appropriate customizations to make the IAM tools work with firewalls, proxy servers, and load balancers.

10. Data migration

    Inappropriate procedures or negligence, while migrating data from one database to another database (which normally happens at the time of mergers and acquisitions), can cause very major risks like cut-over aborts, data redundancy, data loss, data scattering, and injection of unstructured data.

11. Synchronization of data from HR databases to IAM products

    Inappropriate procedures while synchronizing data from a database to an IAM tool can cause major risks and application instability.

Costs and Benefits analysis

Costs and Benefit analysis would be the final step in the strategy generation for IAM products. This stage identifies various costs and benefits involved in IAM product development, sales, support, maintenance, etc. This is the stage in strategy generation which affixes costs for the product and estimates the benefits and profits involved in the product's development.

Costs are directly based on human resources, applications, and technology used in product development. Costs can be categorized into four types as:
1. Fixed costs
2. Variable costs
3. Direct costs
4. Indirect costs

An organization estimates and understands all the above mentioned costs and quotes the price of the identity & access management products (application development or implementation).

Benefit Analysis is the analysis or estimation which should be done prior to service development in order to evaluate and assess the profit margin, benefits, value creation, and brand reputation aspects for the service provider.

Benefits can be further categorized into four types as:
1. Short term benefits
2. Long term benefits
3. Tangible benefits
4. Intangible benefits

Short term benefits are the benefits which are very tangible, which are observed in daily operations, and which yield results in short term.

Long term benefits are the benefits which yield results after a long time duration.

Tangible benefits are the benefits which can be directly associated to a currency value.

Intangible benefits are the benefits which cannot be associated with currency value, but they play a very important role in the development of service like innovation, reputation, etc.

Design for IAM Products

What is Design?

Design is the activity of creating and grouping different related and interrelated components together for making it fit for some purpose. It is the sequence of activities which defines and frames an acceptable solution with the help of various subcomponents (processes, technologies, architectural diagrams, model diagrams, and documentation), criteria, constraints, boundaries, and interfaces.

Design for IAM Product Development

Design for IAM product development can be defined as the definition and development of prototypes/skeleton for identity & access management products, processes, or solutions.
Design for IAM product development can be developed through the below mentioned tasks in a step by step approach:

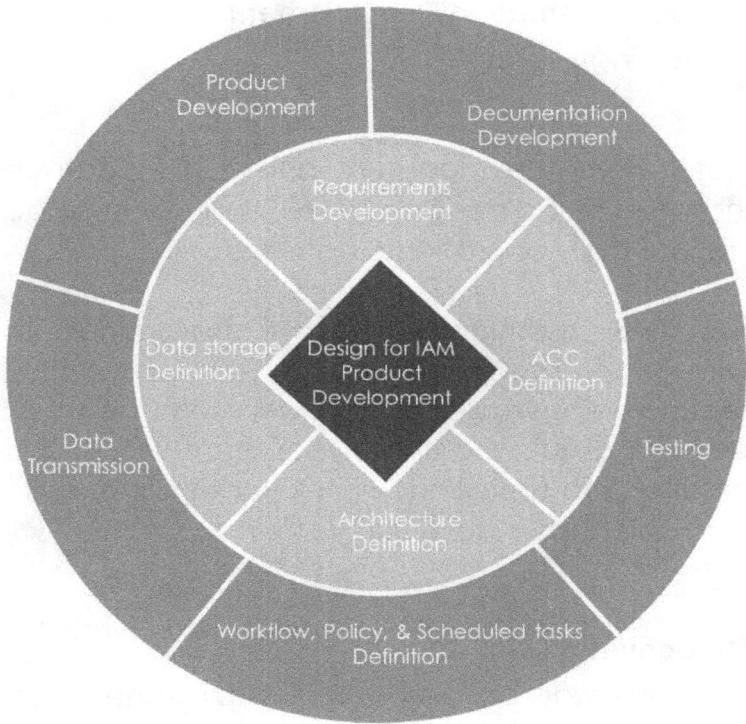

Fig 7: Design for IAM product development

1. Scope definition
2. Requirements Development
3. Availability, Capacity, and Continuity(ACC) Definition
4. Architecture Definition
5. Data storage definition
6. Data transmission
7. Workflow , Policy, and Scheduled tasks definition
8. Product Development

9. Documentation Development
10. Testing

Note: Here, development and testing activities are included in the design phase because these activities are not daily operational activities.

Normally, Technical Architects and Business Analysts with good knowledge on IAM, ITSM applications and technologies would be considered as the best bet to perform requirements development, ACC definition, architecture definition, workflow definition, policy and scheduled tasks definition.

Objectives
- To provide an overview and plan the design with respect to capabilities and limitations.
- To identify the risks and issues in the development of the IAM products or solutions.
- To check the feasibility whether the products/solutions can address and fix customer's requirements.
- To visualize the look and feel of the solution.

Best Practices for Design

- Implement an iterative approach for design activities.
- Usage of best practices defined in ALM, TOGAF, etc.
- Documentation of learning from the previous experiences.
- Consult the key stakeholders while making important decisions.
- Usage of the right resources (with right skills) in the right activities.

Scope Development

Development of scope is the primary and most important step for process development; the main objective of scope development is to define the boundaries for product development work.

Scope development is the activity which comprises:

1. Scope planning
2. Scope definition
3. Scope verification

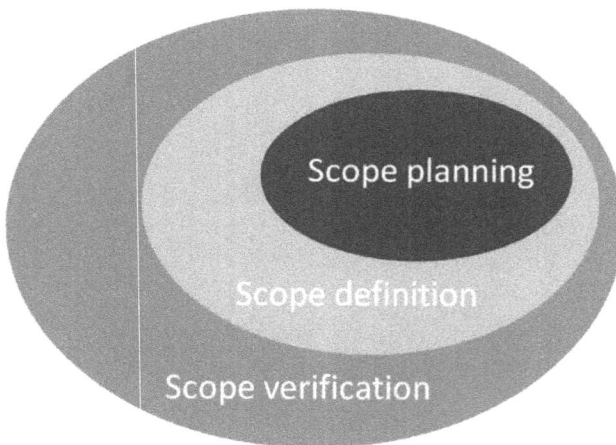

Scope development

Fig 8: Scope Development

Scope planning

Scope planning defines the goals and objectives of a project, identifies the project participants, and gives an overview of the concept development work (which is technically feasible). It also involves defining a product's characteristics (functional and non-functional), objectives of different modules in a product, deliverables, etc.

Scope definition

Scope definition defines the interfaces and boundaries for product development work in terms of scoping and out of scope.

- In-scope or scoping defines different tasks and activities that are managed by the IAM products.
- Out of scope defines the miscellaneous tasks and activities that are not managed by the IAM products.

Scope verification

Scope verification defines the procedure for verifying, validating, and accepting of the scope as defined by the stakeholders (sponsor, client, customer, etc.). It involves reviewing the inputs, deliverables, and expected outcomes to ensure that all the assumptions and estimations are meeting customer's expectations.

Scope development ensures that all key stakeholders understand the scope of the process, project goals, and the statement of work as documented. It also plays a very important role in estimation of the time period, costs, resources, and skills required for developing the process.

Human resources involved in scope definition should possess good understanding of the IAM process, ITSM domain knowledge, and project management knowledge.

Requirements Development

Requirements development is a very important activity which lays the foundation for the complete product delivery which either makes or breaks the product. Requirements development gathers the requirements on the complete product, sets the prerequisites, and defines the criteria for different activities like coding, documentation development, testing, implementation, operations, maintenance, and support. Requirements development for IAM products involves:

1. Requirements gathering
2. Requirements analysis
3. Requirements specification
4. Requirements acceptance review
5. Requirements consolidation

Requirements for IAM product design can be categorized into four types as:
   a. Business requirements
   b. Functional requirements
   c. User requirements
   d. Non-functional requirements

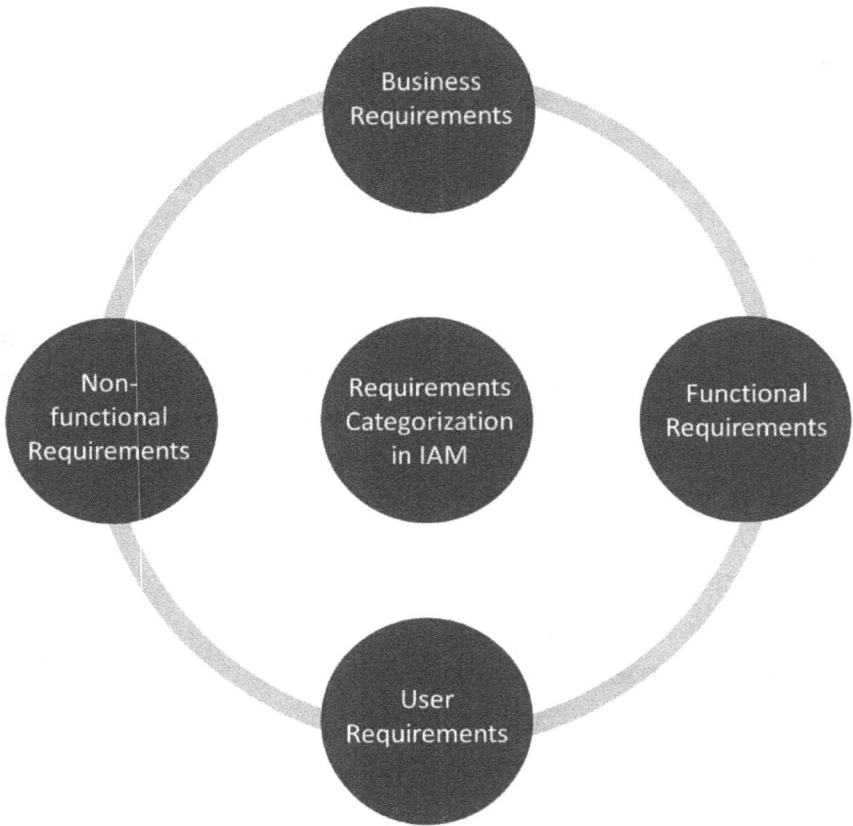

Fig 9: Requirements categorization in IAM

Business requirements

Business requirements represent the business needs/customer needs and business priorities supported by problem areas or pain points in an existing business.

Business requirements for IAM solutions can be mentioned as below:

166

- IAM solution must support and manage a total number of 10,000 users, and it should be scalable to support the increasing number of users.
- IAM solution should manage the end to end lifecycle of user identities and access privileges.

Functional requirements

Functional requirements represent the different features and functionalities needed for IAM solution like:

- IAM application should integrate with existing IT tools (E.g. Service-now ITSM tool, etc.) and applications.
- IAM application should integrate with directory services tools like Microsoft Active Directory, etc.
- IAM application should integrate with existing authentication systems and protocols to authenticate users, processes, and services.

User requirements

User requirements define what users require from the system; it would represent the software solution with respect to different users, considering different roles and profiles.

Non-functional requirements

Non-functional requirements would represent the non-functional requirements of the software solution like look and feel aspects (colours, user interface controls size, font size, font colours, screen resolution considerations, etc.).

Key Essentials for Requirements

Key essentials for requirements can be described through Completeness, Correctness, and Traceability.

Completeness
- *All requirements written at an appropriate level of detail.*
- *Functional requirements provide an adequate basis for design.*
- *All business and functional requirements should have a priority allocation.*
- *Requirements should include all of the customer needs.*

Correctness
- *Requirements should be free from typos, grammatical errors, etc.*
- *Requirements should be clear, concise with adequate diagrams, etc.*
- *Requirements shouldn't conflict with other requirements.*

Traceability
- *All requirements should uniquely identified.*
- *All requirements should have the ability to link with each other.*

Generic functional and technical requirements for IAM solutions are:

- Should support running on various platforms, particularly UNIX or Linux.
- Should be able to import and export identities from different identity sources and sinks.
- Should allow configuration of user session controls to meet security and privacy needs.
- Should integrate with existing IT tools and applications to manage groups, roles, and permissions.
- Must support end-to-end logging for the purposes of diagnostics, statistics collection, and auditing.
- Must allow for secure deployment of IAM components to various tiers of the network. In particular, some authentication components must be deployed to the DMZ to support external services. Therefore, the host operating environment and the applications providing these services must have a history of excellent security and security practices.
- Must support highly-available and high-performance configurations, including clustering, load balancing, and horizontally scalable configurations.
- Must support component isolation, minimally through operating system mechanisms or physically distinct networked nodes.

169

- Should support deployment in a virtualized environment, such that multiple instances of different operating systems can coexist on a single physical node.
- Should support software management mechanisms to aid deployment and maintenance of components distributed across many host nodes.
- Must support integration with both host-based and network-based Intrusion Detection Systems (IDS).
- Should support integration with both host-based and network-based Intrusion Prevention Systems (IPS).

Availability, Capacity and Continuity (ACC)

Definition

Availability

Availability in simple terms is "the capability of any service or any asset being accessible at the right time (as per the necessity of a user)".

Availability for IAM products is the ability of identity & access management products that is reliable, accessible, easily maintainable, and serviceable.

The availability of an IAM system can be measured by the percentage of time that it works as per the defined customer requirements.

Availability of an identity & access management application can be derived by the formula:

*Availability = (Number of operational hours in a month/ Agreed number of hours to support in a month) * 100.*

Capacity

Capacity in simple terms is "the capability to accommodate certain data in a system".

Capacity for IAM products is the ability to have good performance while accessing the systems (in terms of accessing the identity & access management products/applications) as per defined business requirements.

171

General factors which determine the capacity of an IAM system are latency, response time, service time, throughput, wait time, and number of requests that it can handle at a point in time.

Continuity

Continuity in simple terms is the "The capability to deliver continuous and consistent work without any interruptions".

Continuity for IAM products is the capability of identity & access management products that provides continuous and consistent services through a backup strategy which enables delivery of continuous services even when there is any unpredicted natural disasters or accidents.

Availability, Capacity, and Continuity (ACC) for identity & access management products is very vital and critical. Design for IAM products forecasts the ACC considerations for identity & access management products by understanding the SLAs, number of users using the service, number of depending services, business criticality, etc.

A more detailed explanation is provided below:

1. The number of business units and services which cannot exist without a specific identity & access management product.

For example: An organization that has integrated an access management application with its network server will not be able to access the network if the access management application is down.

2. Financial applications associated with an identity & access management product

    For example: Breakdown of a federated identity & access management application in an organization will impact the suppliers, customers, and other partners, and can create penalizations.

3. The number of business units/users which needs a specific identity & access management product but can also survive even if there is a breakdown for a few hours.

    For example: Breakdown of an identity account management application in an organization will impact the administrators who create, update, and delete IT accounts, but yet it doesn't have that great criticality.

Key artifacts that impact the ACC definition are:

1. Hardware (For example: Storage devices, Memory, Processor, etc.)

2. Software (For example: Middleware, Applications, Databases, Operating systems, Programming language, etc.)

173

3. Technology (For example: Clustering, Load Balancing, Proxy server, Firewall, Partitioning, Backup, etc.)
4. Environment (For example: Power, Space, Temperature, etc.)

Hardware
All physical assets or equipment that are involved in the identity & access management system is categorized as Hardware.

Software
All programs enabling the hardware to work in the identity & access management system is categorized as Software.

Technology
Technology is the topology of the hardware, software, and various methods used by hardware and software which makes the identity & access management system work.

Clustering

It is the arrangement of many computers or servers that work together but is viewed as a single system. It is the concept of providing data redundancy to enable better availability. Clustering can be implemented in two ways: Cold failover cluster and Active failover cluster.

174

Cold failover cluster (CFC): In CFC arrangement, one machine is in active state carrying out operations, while another machine is in a standby state. When there is any kind of breakdown from the active machine, the other machine in standby status is initiated immediately and carries out the work ensuring high availability.

Active failover cluster (AFC): In AFC arrangement, both machines are in active status carrying out operations or performing services ensuring better availability.

Load balancing

It is the arrangement of computers or servers that will share the workload of an information system or database to maximize throughput, minimize workload on IT components, and decrease response time for users. Load balancing is implemented using different algorithms like round robin, weighted round robin, least connections, and least response time.

Proxy server

It is the arrangement of computers or servers that will protect the application hosted servers from any security risks and threats. The proxy server acts as a mediator between client and server or between two networks providing the below mentioned advantages like:

- Obnubilation of client IP address
- Restricting specific websites
- Logging and tracking the accessed web pages

Proxy servers can be categorized into three types as Reverse proxy server, Forward proxy server, and Open proxy server.

Reverse proxy server is a proxy server that accesses network resources from different destination servers or internet and passes it to its clients or internal network; Reverse proxy servers doesn't require any client side configuration.

Forward proxy server is a proxy server which forwards the requests from internal network or client machines to destination servers or the internet.

Open proxy server is a proxy server that can forward requests from and to anywhere on the internet.

Partitioning
It is the arrangement of computers or servers that will partition the server into two or more parts and

assign specific tasks to perform, which reduces the burden on a server.

Backup
It is the arrangement of multiple computers or servers so that the data is mirrored at another or different locations to provide continuity when there is any breakdown of service from the primary machine.

Environment
Environment is the external artifacts like temperature, and space conditions that enable the IAM products run efficiently.

Effective availability for identity & access management products can be defined by:

Reliability
Reliability defines the continuous operations of the identity & access management products without any breakdown or interruption.

Maintainability
Maintainability defines the adaptable architecture of an identity & access management product which is scalable or repairable. Maintainability of an IAM products can be depicted through the number of

177

hours taken to perform any maintenance works like upgrades, migrations, etc.

Serviceability
Serviceability is the warranty services provided for an identity & access management product.

Effective capacity for identity & access management products can be defined by:

Throughput
Throughput is defined by the number of transactions performed by a server in a fixed time.

Application Sizing Methods
Application sizing methods estimates the intended capacity (performance) requirements for an application to support any major changes like an increase in number of users, integration with new applications, upgrades of the application, etc.

Tuning Methods
Tuning methods defines different ways to improve the performance related issues on an application.

Effective continuity for an identity & access management products can be defined by:

Rollback methods
Rollback method defines how to restore an

178

application when a specific change did not achieve the expected results.

Backup methods
Backup method defines how the data is backed up or mirrored in the same location (onsite) or another location (offsite) as a precautionary measure.

Critical Success Factors (CSFs) for ACC definition

- Understand the business requirements with respect to ACC considerations from customer stakeholders (management and also technical teams).
- Understand technical requirements with respect to ACC from the technical team
- Check any existing information systems ACC configuration, utilization rate, number of users using the system effectively, number of users using the system randomly, costs incurring, user satisfaction, etc.
- Contact the technologists who had experience in defining ACC for IAM systems.
- Test the designed ACC parameters before the IAM tools are live.
- Develop remediation plans, forecasting the increase in number of users during natural disasters.

Architecture Definition

Architecture in simple terms is a design or skeleton of a system; software architecture can be defined as "the arrangement of different internal components (which represents the communication flow, relationships, internal dependencies, roles, etc.) that makes a meaningful and purposeful design, also establishing guidelines and procedures for developing a software product".

The idea of defining architecture for identity & access management products should begin with:

- Business Architecture
- Application Architecture
- Data Architecture
- Technology Architecture

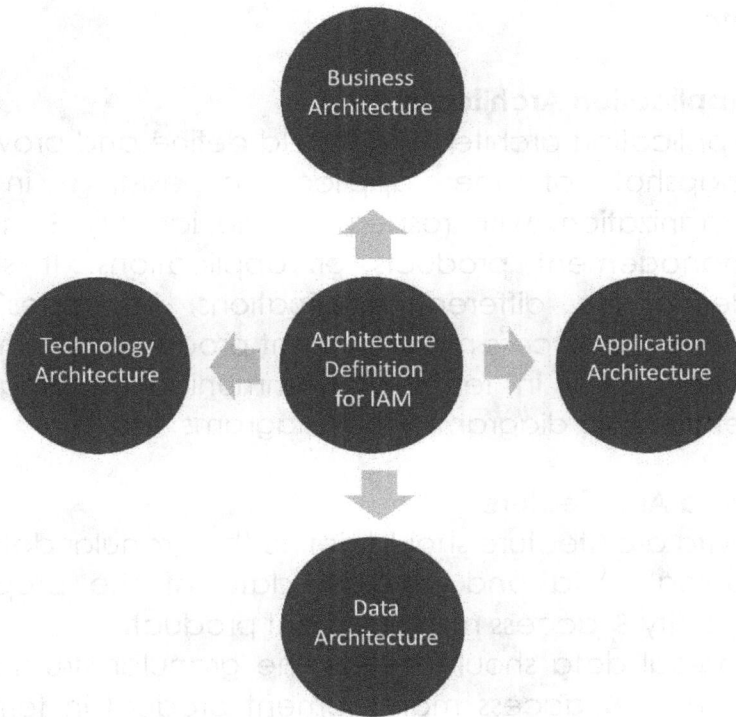

Fig 10: Types of architecture in IAM

Business Architecture

Business architecture should define and provide a snapshot of the business processes involved in an organization, with respect to the identity & access management process.

It should identify all the different organizational business processes, identity & access management processes in terms of communication diagrams, relationship diagrams, role diagrams, goal diagrams,

181

etc.

Application Architecture

Application architecture should define and provide a snapshot of the applications existing in the organization, with respect to the identity & access management products or applications. It should define the different applications, interfaces and identity & access management products defining the functionality in terms of communication diagrams, relationship diagrams, goal diagrams, etc.

Data Architecture

Data architecture should define the granular details of logical data and physical data of the proposed identity & access management product.

Logical data should define the granular structure of identity & access management product in terms of class diagrams, communication diagrams, relationship diagrams, role diagrams, goal diagrams, etc.

Physical data should define the granular details of identity & access management product in terms of forms, User Interface (UI) controls, tables, data types, data length, validations, etc.

Technology Architecture

Technology architecture should define and provide a snapshot of the technology related elements, its importance, and its functionality in identity & access management system. It involves the arrangement of components like databases, application servers, web servers, middleware, operating systems, front end, proxy server, clusters, remote servers, hardware configuration, etc.

Critical Success Factors (CSFs) for Architecture definition

- Alignment of architecture design as per the business and user requirements.
- Performing risk analysis throughout the architecture design.
- Effective tools for designing architectural diagrams.
- Evaluation of the architecture deliverables at regular intervals.
- Skilled team with experience in architecting, coding, testing and business analysis.
- Definition of architecture as per the industry best practices like The Open Group Architecture Framework (TOGAF), Generalized Enterprise Reference Architecture and Methodology (GERAM), etc.

Data Storage Definition

Data storage in simple terms is storing data for future purposes which would be stored for a stipulated short period of time (temporarily) or for a long term (permanently).

Storage of the identity & access management data can be categorized in two ways:
● Database storage
● Directory storage

Database storage
In database storage approach, all data related to user identity information is stored in database tables in the form of rows and columns.
This approach is very much familiar for all of us; this methodology uses different concepts like data types, normalization rules, data definition languages, data manipulation languages, data control languages, data persistence, etc.
Examples: Oracle database, SQL database, etc.

Directory storage
In directory storage approach, only some of the user identity data and information (roles, user specific credentials, user title, shared resources, etc.) is stored

in directories.

This approach stores the data in the form of directory entries arranged in the Directory Information Tree (DIT). DIT provides a structure for arranging the directory data using attribute index values for ease of accessibility.

Examples: Active Directory, Oracle Internet Directory, etc.

Comparisons between database and directory server

Database holds the data in tables (in the form of rows and columns).

Database storage is commonly used for actions like read, write, edit, and delete.

Directory holds the data in DIT (in the form of directory entries).

Directory storage is commonly used when the data is mostly read.

Data Transmission

Data transmission in simple terms is transfer of data from one system to another system.

Data transmission in identity & access management systems can happen through programming languages, scripting languages, extensible markup languages, and database languages. Commonly used protocols for data transmissions in identity & access management systems are LDAP (Lightweight directory access protocol), SSH (Secure shell), and Telnet.

LDAP: LDAP is a lightweight directory access application protocol for maintaining and managing information in directory servers.

SSH: SSH is secure shell application protocol for secure communication between two networked computers.

Telnet: Telnet is a bidirectional text-oriented communication protocol for remote users.

Common extensible markup languages used in identity & access management systems communications are DSML, DAML, SAML, SPML, XACML, WSS, OAuth, and Open ID.

Directory Services Markup Language

DSML is a markup language which enables the users to represent directory information in XML. With the latest

186

version DSML v2, users can perform various operational tasks like sending queries and making updates to the directory servers using XML.

DSML v2 can be primarily categorized into two documents: Request documents and Response documents.

Request documents are the documents sent by the client to the server.

Response documents are the documents sent by the server to the client.

Directory Access Markup Language

DAML is an XML specification that represents the directory operations. DAML extends the functionalities of DSML.

Security Assertion Markup Language (SAML)

SAML is an XML based language used for communicating authentication and authorization information as assertions between different applications and identity & access management systems.

Main components of SAML are Assertions, Request/Response Protocol, Bindings and Profiles.

SAML uses three types of statements:

1. Authentication statements
2. Attribute statements
3. Authorization decision statements

With respect to the three SAML statements there are three types of queries:

1. Authentication query

2.   Attribute query
3.   Authorization decision query

Service Provisioning Markup Language (SPML)
SPML is another XML based language for communicating the provisioning information for different IT resources and users (SPML is based on DSML v2).
SPML enables the identity & access management system to setup user interfaces (which includes creating, updating, revoking, etc.) easily and quickly for various applications and IT resources. SPML uses three primary roles for provisioning the user interfaces:
1.   Requesting Authority (an entity that makes a request)
2.   Provisioning Service Provider (an entity that responds to the requests)
3.   Provisioning Service Target (an entity that performs the provisioning)

Extensible Access Control Markup Language (XACML)
XACML is another XML based language for managing and controlling the access control and authorization requests. XACML can provide PBAC (Policy Based Access Control), ABAC (Attribute Based Access Control), and RBAC (Role Based Access Control) for users and IT resources.
XACML uses the same definitions as SAML for defining an organization's security policies and for access and

authorization requests.

Web Services Security (WSS)

Web services security specification defines a set of standard simple object access protocol (SOAP) extensions to allow the implementation of integrity and confidentiality in web services applications. WSS provides the foundation for secure web services which provide additional benefits like federation, policy, and trust.

Workflows, Policies and Scheduled Tasks Definition

Workflow

Workflow is a predefined repeatable procedures that defines and manages a sequence of activities and approvals which yields to specific outcomes.

Workflows enable applications to manage and execute certain tasks and decisions in a consistent way without any explicit efforts needed in decision making.

Some common workflows designed in IAM solutions are:

- Workflow for new employee account creation
- Workflow for employee resignations
- Workflow for self-registration on some applications

Policy

Policy is a defined rule for specific roles or user groups; Roles and User Groups are attested to policies.

Policies enable specific roles to perform specific tasks with the same and streamlined privileges.

Some common policies for IAM solutions are:

- Password policies
- User Identity policies

Scheduled tasks

Scheduled tasks are predefined tasks (like scripts, programs) in an application which are executed automatically at a specific point in time or which are executed at regular intervals.

Scheduled tasks enable automation of tasks without any explicit work needed by a specific role or administrators.

Workflows, Policies, and Scheduled tasks are based on two important artifacts: Events and Roles.

- Events

  Events are any important actions that have importance to the business process.

  For example:

  1. User requesting for an application access
  2. HR sends an employee termination request, etc.

- Roles

  Roles are specific users responsible to perform specific actions in a business process scenario.

  For example: Administrator, Contributor, etc.

Workflows, Policies, and Scheduled tasks are features and requirements that are very much essential for all IAM applications which provide great ease for different kinds of users.

IAM Product Deployment

This stage transforms all consolidated requirements, ACC definitions, architecture definitions, workflows, policies & scheduled tasks definitions into code using appropriate programming languages, scripting languages, XML based languages, and database languages to fulfill business requirements.
This phase can be executed by using different software development methodologies like Waterfall, Incremental, V-model, Agile, etc. as per business and stakeholders' requirements.

IM (Identity management) product deployment in IT infrastructure

Identity management product's primary tasks can be described as provisioning, control, and de-provisioning of IT accounts.

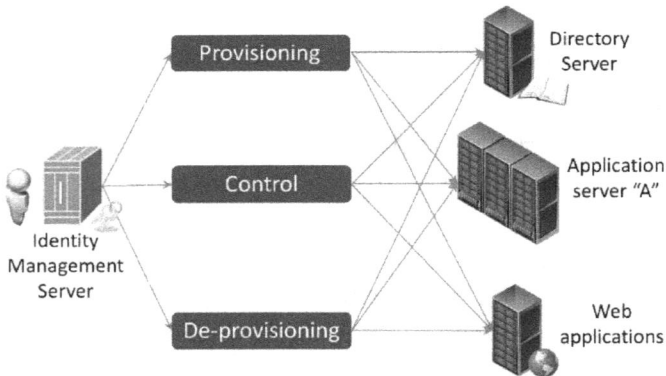

Fig 11: Primary tasks in Identity management

Identity management products interface and integrate with numerous databases, directories, applications, and users in IT environment as shown in the below image:

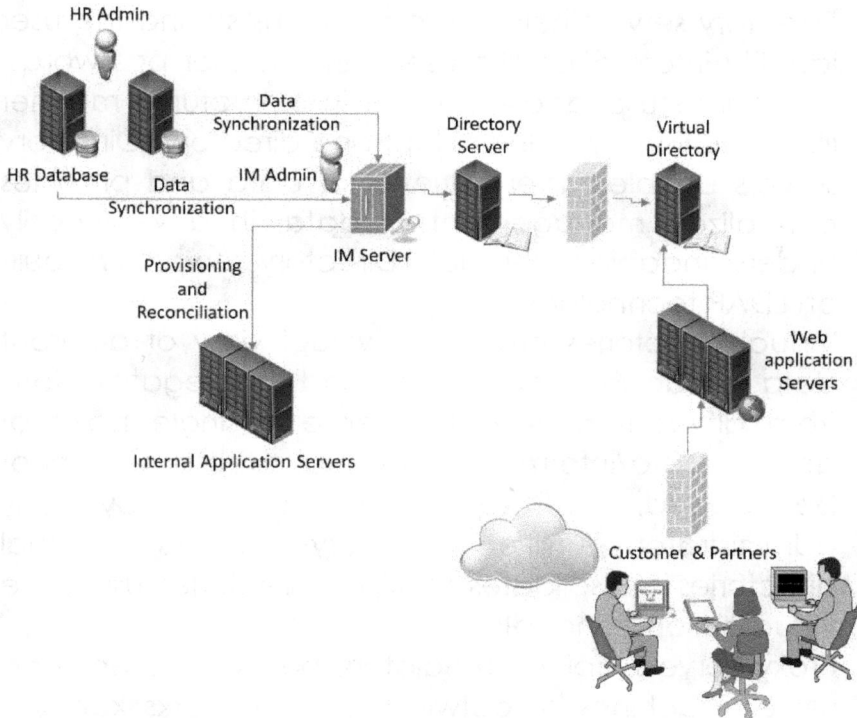

Fig 12: Identity management in IT infrastructure

HR databases stores the human resources (employees, contractors, partners, etc.) information, and this data is synchronized to identity management servers via software programs and migration tools (HR Administrators manages the HR databases).

IM servers help IT organizations in defining unified user

identities, passwords and enables them to do effective provisioning, controlling, and de-provisioning of the user identities for different internal applications, directories, and external applications (IM Admin manages the IM servers).

Directory servers help IT organizations storing the user identity information like user identity, user passwords, user name, user addresses, etc. in a structured manner like a dictionary or like telephone directory (Directory servers enable faster retrieval of data and provides centralized management of data, in a very easily understandable approach. Directory servers are built on LDAP technology).

Virtual directories provide a virtual view of different data databases, directories and aggregates data from different sources to create a single point of access. Data/information in virtual directories cannot be added, updated, and deleted by any administrator unlike directory servers (Virtual directories consolidates multiple directories using the virtualization concepts).

Proxy servers act as mediators between client and server machines or between two networks keeping the server machine's IP address anonymous for better security, protecting it from hackers and threats.

Firewall is software or hardware based network security mechanism that protects the organizational resources (servers) from any attacks from hackers, snoopers, and virus attacks.

Integrated identity and access management products deployment in IT environment

Integrated identity and access management products in IT environment can bring great benefits like:

- Automated provisioning, de-provisioning, and control on IT user accounts
- Precise controls on access (authenticates and authorizes access to internal employees and other public users)

Here is a simulation of how identity management and access management products work together as shown below:

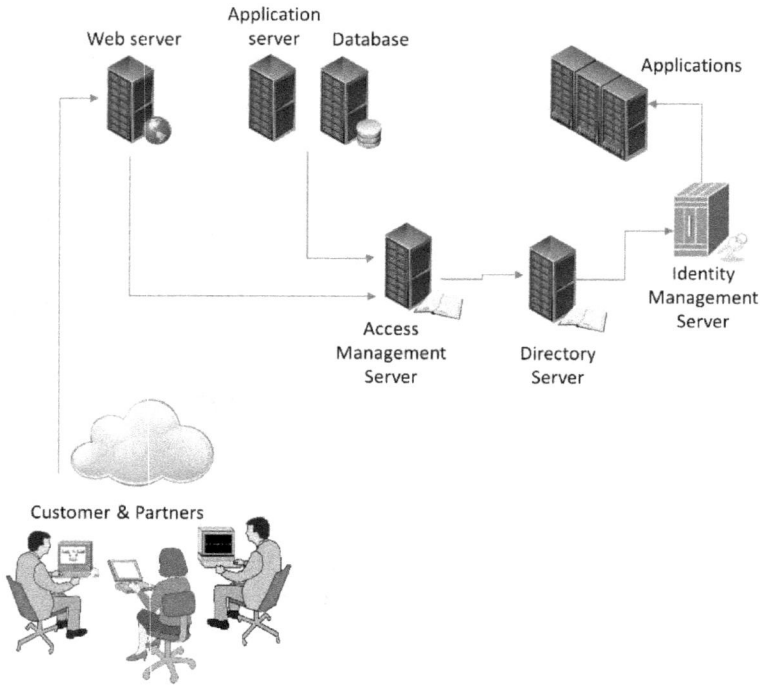

Fig 13: Integrated IAM management in IT infrastructure

Documentation Development

Documentation development is the activity which involves development of documentation deliverables for the IAM product which will enable different types of users to use and manage the IAM solutions. Documentation development can be defined in four stages as mentioned below:

- Planning and Analysis
- Design and Develop
- Review
- Publish

Planning and Analysis
Planning and Analysis stage understands the requirements of the customers and determines what kind of documentation deliverables (user manuals, administration guide, installation guide, release notes, work instructions, help files, etc.) would fulfill the requirements of customers, what are the formats of documentation deliverables (word document, pdf's, etc.), and what is the time and effort required.

Design and Develop
This stage designs and develops documentation deliverables as per the customer's requirements. It involves all activities like defining templates, styles, standards, and developing the content.

197

Review

Review stage reviews the developed documents to ensure that they are easily understandable, user friendly, and provide detailed guidance to work with the application.

Publish

Publish stage publishes the documentation deliverables in the respective formats as a package with the product and deploys it in the customer's environment.

Testing

Testing is the activity for verifying and validating the final IAM product which is to be deployed in the customer's operational environment.

This activity implements different types of testing approaches on developed or customized IAM products.

Some of the important test types that should be performed are:

- Unit testing
- Form level testing
- Functionality testing
- Integration testing
- Regression testing
- System testing
- Operational readiness testing

Unit Testing

Unit testing is an activity where individual units of source code are tested to check if the code is aligning and meeting the business requirements. A unit may be described as an individual function or procedure in IAM. Unit testing is normally performed by programmers or explicit white box testers.

Form level testing

Form level testing is the activity where all individual granular components (UI controls) of form and logics

199

associated with UI controls in the form (as a whole entity) are tested.

Functionality testing
Functionality testing is the activity which tests the functionality of every individual module, every feature provided in the application (workflows, policies, scheduled tasks, notifications, and alerts), and every UI controls in a form.

Integration Testing
Integration testing is the activity which tests communication and integration aspects of all modules and features in IAM applications; it also tests the way how an IAM application communicates and integrates with other external applications.

Regression testing
Regression testing is the activity which retests the application or specific module again after developers fix the defects logged.
The main objective of regression testing is to check if there are any new defects after fixes are implemented.

System Testing
System testing is the activity which tests integrated complete IAM systems to verify and validate whether or not the system is working correctly as planned and meets business requirements.
System testing on IAM applications is implemented by

testing end to end scenarios of different tasks using various roles.

Performance Testing

Performance testing is the activity which checks the IAM system's responsiveness towards user's queries and responsiveness on different configurations (like memory, processor speed, etc.). Performance testing can be classified into two important types: Load Testing and Stress Testing.

Documentation Testing

Documentation testing is the activity which verifies and validates all of the documentation deliverables to see:

- whether or not they are in sync with the product functionality
- whether or not the documentation can guide users to use the product and perform different tasks
- whether or not the documentation instructions and language is easily understandable

Operational Readiness Testing

Operational readiness testing is the activity which happens before the implementation of an IAM product in the customer's environment.
This testing will ensure that the product is fit for use in an operational environment (customer's/ organizational) with all features like checking the

disaster recovery procedures, backup facilities, back out plan, remediation plan, etc.

Proof of Concept (POC)

Proof of concept is the implementation and demonstration of IAM products and its services in a customer's environment (it may also involve a small number of live users and few applications) to win confidence and to showcase the functionality & benefits of developed IAM services or products.

Objectives of POC for IAM tools are:
- To understand the installation, deployment and operations of an IAM tool in a pragmatic approach.
- To determine if the IAM tool would integrate with other IS's in organization.
- To check if the processes in IAM tools can integrate with other business processes defined.
- To evaluate business benefits that can be obtained by an IAM tool.

Some organizations consider POC (Proof of Concept) as an activity part of sales, and some consider it as a preliminary milestone of the implementation phase. The success of POC will decide whether the customer would buy the product/services.
POC can also be considered as a small project which

normally runs for about 2-3 weeks. A service provider would plan and implement the POC through:

- Requirement analysis
- Scenario design
- Scenario development
- Scenario test
- POC reporting

Generally, POC is normally demonstrated by the best engineers of a service provider; as it is the most challenging task because of the time constraints. POC will not only challenge the products quality, reliability, and usability, it also challenges the skills and abilities of human resources to provide the solution in less amount of time.

Best practices for conducting POC with respect to IAM tools are:

- Involvement of the best human resources in POC whom have adept knowledge in IAM technology, processes, and IT infrastructure components (Active Directory, Databases, Directories, Applications, etc.).
- Demonstration of POC shouldn't take more than a month (maximum).
- Timeframe for a POC should be well planned and in proportion to the actual implementation of the IAM products.

- Inclusion of testing methods like user acceptance testing (through customer stakeholders), performance testing, load testing, and stress testing.
- Deliverables of a POC should also include product specific FAQs, roles and responsibilities, product training, FRS (Functional Requirement Specification), TRS (Technical Requirement Specification), and use cases.

Implementation

Implementation in simple terms is the execution of the developed product in a real environment.

Implementation of identity & access management system refers to deployment and operations of identity & access management system in an organization with real data and users.

A few important measures before implementing a new identity & access management solution in an organization are:

1. Identify the types of users (fulltime and part time employees, contractors, partners, suppliers) and consolidate the identities.

2. Identify the information systems that they have access to?

3. Determine from where the IAM system should obtain data?

4. Determine how the data should be synchronized?

5. Validate the software and hardware configurations prior to deployment.

6. Implement IAM system with AD environment.

7. Identify and document the risks, issues, & lessons learned in IAM and AD integration.

8. Identify the other information systems which have to be integrated with IAM system.
9. Design the architecture for IAM and other respective information systems.
10. Integrate IAM products with other information systems.
11. Evaluate the identity & access management product in a test environment which mirrors the production environment.
12. Define and test the rollback plan.
13. Rollout the identity & access management product in a phased approach (for a specific number of users, for a specific application, etc.) - never try a big bang approach.
14. Perform complete product testing after deployment.
15. Define enough documentation (User Manuals, Administration Guide, and Installation Guide) for usage of the identity & access management product.
16. Develop a knowledge base with all the technical issues faced and how they were resolved at the time of development and testing.

Key aspects to be considered while selecting an IAM tools

IAM tool implementation in an organization involves huge costs, time, and effort; It can either make the organization's business run more effectively and efficiently or create new problems, great risks, and non-compliance issues leading to penalizations and loss of reputation. A few important necessities to be considered before selecting any IAM tools are:

- Functionality of the tool
  IAM tool selection should be based on the core functionality of the product. Functionality of IAM tools/applications can be understood by:
  1. Understanding the process diagrams, free trial versions, information brochures, and other documentation.
  2. Meetings with the sales team.
  3. Demonstrations of the products and POC.

- Features of the tool
  Important features to be provided in IAM tool are:
  1. Automated provisioning and de-provisioning of user accounts
  2. Reconciliation of user accounts
  3. Segregation of duties

4. Workflow systems
5. Ability to support different data repositories
6. Review and certification systems

- Technology of the tool
Technology also plays a very important role in IAM application selection as IAM applications integrate and communicate with various applications and databases in an organization. Selection of any IAM application with some obsolete and inefficient technology can lead to numerous issues like increases in cost, time, complexity, etc.

- Performance of the tool
Performance of the IAM applications is the ability to respond to user queries and actions. Performance of IAM applications can be determined by:
1. Page load speed
2. Number of transactions per second

- Infrastructure needed by the tool
Infrastructure also a plays very important role in the

IAM application which is based on:

1. Organization's Hardware, Software (existing applications, databases, middleware and operating systems), People-ware (Employees, Partners and Suppliers)
2. Enterprise and IT architecture

- Support for customization
Ability to customize the IAM applications as per changing demands and requirements of the organization would provide great value for investments made by the organization. Customization features should be mainly available on:
1. UI controls
2. Workflows
3. Policies
4. Support to open standards

- Scalability
IAM applications should have the capability to scale itself as per the various requirements like an increase in number of users and increase in the number of applications and databases. Scalability for IAM applications can be done either by scaling up resources (adding more memory, processor, etc.) or scaling out (adding more computers to share the loads) methods.

- Workflows

  IAM applications should be equipped with effective workflows which should enable automation of routine tasks and help in making effective decisions.

- Search features

  Search features would be a great value for IAM applications by making data and information visible, traceable, and accessible in quick time. Applications should provide features like:
  1. Creation of customized search functions
  2. Ability to search data in specific silos in IAM system
  3. Ability to search data in complete IAM system
  4. Ability to search objects, workflows, and policies
  5. Ability to search documents and images

- Accessibility from portable devices

  Considering the trends in information technology, IAM applications should be developed in such a way that they are accessible even from mobile devices like smart phones, PDA's, gadgets, etc.

- Provision for integration with 3rd party applications

Provision for integrating IAM applications with 3rd party applications like AD (Active Directory), Email systems, and other applications with less complexity, in less time, and efficiently is another aspect which can gain great value for the IAM service provider and organizations using the applications. Provision for integrating IAM applications to 3rd party applications can be done by developing connectors.

Connectors are the technical pieces of code which acts as a liaison between two or more applications and communicates the information between different applications.

- Business Intelligence and Analytics
  Business Intelligence and Analytics is the discovery and analysis of organizations important meaningful data (with statistical methods) and communicating it to the stakeholders for making effective decisions.

- Reporting features
  Reporting is another important feature needed by the IAM application administrators which enables it in creating different types of reports for different levels of management.

- User friendliness

  User friendliness is another important aspect for applications selection which can be determined by the features like:

  1. WYSIWYG feature
  2. Web interface and Windows application interface
  3. Easy to navigate
  4. GUI (Graphical User Interface)
  5. Easy to troubleshoot
  6. Easy to install and maintain
  7. Provision of enough documentation

Operations for IAM Products

What is Operations?

Operations are the daily, routine activities that are involved in any specific work.

Operations for Identity & Access Management

Operations for identity & access management can be defined as the daily, routine activities that are involved in maintaining identity & access management systems to meet the organizational business requirements. Operations for identity & access management ensure that the identity & access management product/solution is continuously running effectively and efficiently and meets the business requirements. Operational activities in identity & access management system involve many routine tasks like user account management, access governance, account provisioning and de-provisioning, reconciliation, accounts certification and recertification, auditing, and some generic tasks like database administration, datacenter management, backup, restoration, etc.

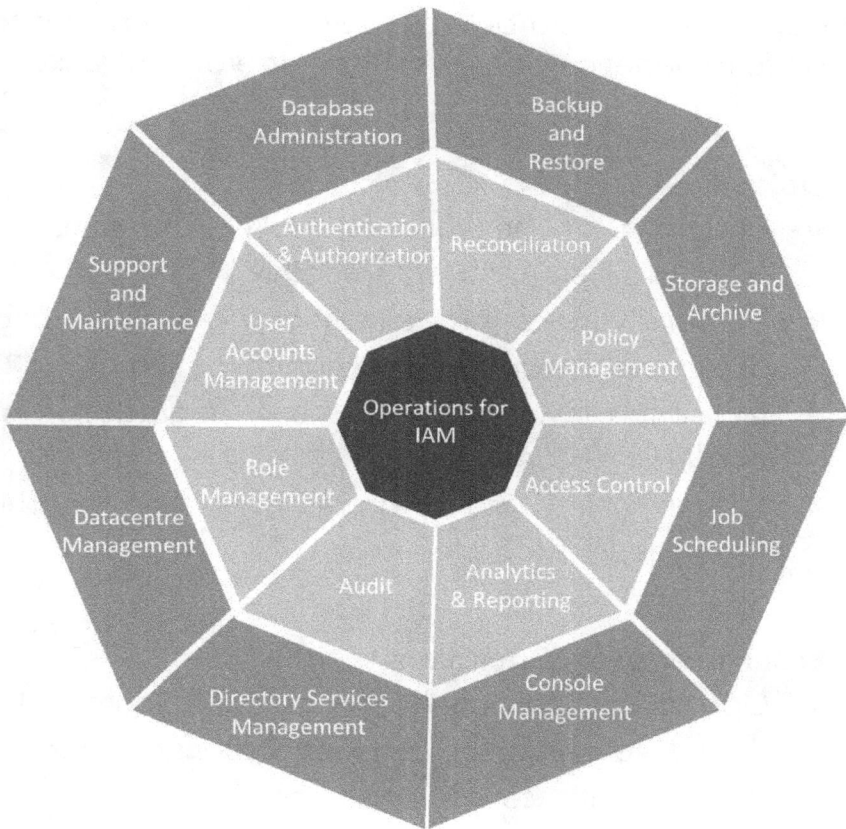

Fig 14: Operations for IAM

IAMS categorizes operational activities of identity & access management systems into 2 types:

- Generic operational activities
- IAM Specific operational activities

Normally Operational Level Management like Team Leaders, System Administrators, and Operations Analysts with knowledge on IT infrastructure and IAM applications would be considered as the best bet to perform generic and IAM specific operational tasks.

Objectives

- Execution of the services (daily operations) in production environment smoothly.
- To identify issues (proactively and reactively) and determine the appropriate control action.
- To reduce any breakdowns and degradation of quality in services.
- To identify any kind of failures, issues and report it to the design stage for fixes.

Best Practices for Operations

- Operations contacts list prepared (IT Contacts list should have the summary of responsible people for a specific service, with their name, contact number, email id, contact time).
- Understanding of SLAs, SLOs, UCs, OLAs with its stakeholders.
- Awareness on IS policies and procedures
- Effective utilization of resources and their skills.
- Should have customer oriented staff.

Generic operational activities

Generic operational activities are generic for all IT systems which can be stated as:

1. Database administration
2. Backup and Restore
3. Storage and Archive
4. Job Scheduling
5. Console management
6. Directory services management
7. Data center management
8. Service desk support
9. Onsite support

Database administration

Database administration is the activity of maintaining and managing the databases used in the identity & access management system with optimum performance, availability, and security standards.
It involves many tasks like:

- Designing the database
- Administration of database objects
- Monitoring the usage on response time, transaction volumes, etc.
- Generating reports

217

Backup and Restore

Backup is a method of copying all the identity & access management systems data and saving at another location – thereby, being prepared for any unexpected situations. Backup is a method based on the concepts of data redundancy; it can be done in different models as Full backup, Partial backup, Incremental backup, etc.

Restore is a method of restoring or reconstructing the same data (as it is) when data is lost by any accidents caused by humans or natural disasters.

Storage and Archive

Storage and archive is another concept which sounds very close to Backup and Restore; But Storage and Archive is an activity of storing data and ensuring that data is stored in the appropriate way with the right technology, right place, with right policies, in the right format, and accessible for right people.

Job Scheduling

Job scheduling is an automated task/activity performed by a software application to save time and reduce manual efforts. Generally it performs activities like approvals, report creations, etc.

Job scheduling helps in:

- Reducing errors
- Eliminating manual work
- Reducing the time consumption

Console management

Console management provides single point of view for administering, controlling, managing various events, alerts, notifications, warnings, and exceptions triggered by the identity & access management technology components.

Directory services management

Directory service management is the management of objects or resources in a directory server; it is arranged in a dictionary like structure. Directory services are based on protocols like DAP (Directory Access Protocol) and LDAP (Lightweight Directory Access Protocol).

Data center management

Datacenter management is the team managing the data centers appropriately and ensuring that the servers are monitored regularly with respect to performance and availability, maintained with right environmental conditions, with right power supply, and ensuring that the services are running appropriately in the data centers.

Service desk support

Service desk support is the team which acts like a SPOC for users on the phone, for issues like failure of a service/application/database or reduction in the quality of an IAM service, and other frequently occurring issues like password reset, account lockout, general information, etc.

Onsite Support

Onsite support is the team which sends onsite technicians for technical and complicated issues that were not solved by service desk support.

IAM Operational Activities

User Accounts management

User Accounts Management is the process of creating, maintaining, controlling, and deleting the user accounts, groups (An object which is a collection of homogeneous user accounts), and entitlements.

User Account: A unique identifier which represents a user to use and perform specific actions on an information system.

Groups: A collection of user accounts which have the same privileges and entitlements.

Entitlements: Set of privileges that can be associated with a user account to perform specific actions in an information system.

Primary details needed for User Accounts Management are:

Employee Full Name (First Name, Middle Name, and Last Name)
Employee Display Name
Account Name
Employee Start Date
Employee End Date
Employee ID
Employee Type (Full-time, Contractor, Intern, etc.)
User Type (End-user, Administrator, Super user)
Job Title
Office Phone

Mobile Phone

Address

Office Location

Manager name

Department (Employee who is a part of specific department)

Organization name

Role Management

Role management is the process of creating, maintaining, controlling, deleting roles, and managing SOD (Segregation of Duties) in identity and access management system. Role management simplifies the alignment of user access with the job function and access request processes.

Role: Roles define the authority and responsibility of a user in an information system. Roles are associated with the IT user's accounts in the information system. As administrators are continuously involved in provisioning user accounts for all their stakeholders, a definition of roles and assignment of the users to the respective roles makes an administrator's job very easy and also provides a structured and streamlined management of user accounts.

SOD (Segregation of Duties): SOD exists as a provision of clarity in roles and responsibilities while performing a task with different roles in identity and access management system.

Primary details needed for Role Management are:

Role Name

Role Display Name
Role Description
Permissions (Create, Modify, Delete, etc.)
Role Category
Role email id
Role Owner
Role members

Authentication and Authorization

Authentication is a security mechanism for identifying and checking who the end-user is and with respect to data stored. Authentication enables an administrator to identify a user with unique credentials which will enable a user to access a service or services.

Authorization is a security mechanism which grants permission to authenticated user/users to do something or to access a service. Authorization is preceded by authentication; Authentication and Authorization involves some services like password management, password synchronization, multifactor authentication, SSO, OTP, etc.

Password Management: Password management is the management of passwords which involves password hardening (defining policies for setting up strong passwords), password maintenance (password changing policies), and password recovery procedures (when the user forgets the password).

SSO: SSO (Single Sign-on Service) is a method which enables the user to login once with a single password and access many resources.

Remote Sign On: The ability of identities to access the IT resources/services from a remote location or outside the organization. This type of remote access should occur in a very secure way through VPN's.

Password Synchronization: This is a method which enables administrators to synchronize passwords in the application credential databases so that users and applications do not have to explicitly change passwords for every application.

OTP: OTP (One Time Password) is a method which generates a temporary password at the time of first login or when a user forgets the password; as the name mentions, this password can be used only once.

Multifactor authentication: The procedure of authenticating a user twice or more using USB tokens, smartcards, biometrics and traditional login credentials to enable stronger security for IS or organizational assets.

Access control

Access is the ability of a user to use and perform specific actions on an information system. Access control is the selective restriction of access and monitoring activity on user's access privileges to ensure that they have access to only necessary information systems or only specific areas in the information system - nothing extra and nothing less.

Access control is in charge of the decision making process for access request by verifying:

● Role assigned to the user

- Organization/Department of the user

Access control improves accuracy of user access assignment and streamlines user access request process. Access control can be automated and managed through the definition of policies and workflows.

The six most important access control models are:

DAC (Discretionary Access Control) is the provisioning of access defined and configured by the owner of an object in IAM systems. The data owner determines the access control based on his knowledge with respect to the requirements.

MAC (Mandatory Access Control) is the provisioning of access to specific resources on services based on criteria which is set as mandatory.

ABAC (Attribute Based Access Control) is the provisioning of access to specific resources on services and based on the attributes of a role or user.

RBAC (Role Based Access Control) is the provisioning of access to specific resources on services, depending on the roles defined in IAM. It is also called non-discretionary access control.

PBAC (Policy-based Access control) is the provisioning of access to specific resources on services, depending on the policies defined in IAM. Policies are the conditions set on users and roles, and it can also address attributes of resources, users, sessions, etc.

RBAC (Risk Based Access Control) is the provisioning of access based on the risks associated with a transaction. Risk based access control is closely associated with authentication.

Access Certification: This is a periodic review on user entitlements to ensure there are no discrepancies in access granting.

Primary details needed for User Access Control are:

Attribute Name

Role Name

Rule name

Policy Name (which can be categorized as Authentication, Authorization, Protected resource, Public resource, User, Group, etc.)

Permissions

Reconciliation

Reconciliation is the process of copying and synchronizing the information (user accounts information) from a database to an identity management system or identity management system to a database.

There are two types of reconciliations:

Trusted Source Reconciliation: A database or a repository is considered as a trusted source, and its data is reconciled into IAM system. This process of reconciliation can be done either as Full or Incremental reconciliation.

Target Source Reconciliation: Data in an IAM system is reconciled into a database or repository. This process of reconciliation is done as a Full reconciliation and only once.

Primary details needed for reconciliation are:
Reconciliation Name
Reconciliation Status
Reconciliation type (Trusted source, Target source)
Reconciliation last performed (date and time)
Reconciliation last performed by
Reconciliation interval (Daily, Weekly, Monthly)
Port No.
Server address

Audit

Audit is the process of validation on IAM data to capture, monitor, report the non-compliances, and ensure that data is maintained with confidentiality, integrity, and non-repudiation.

Auditing validates the data in terms of User Profile Auditing, Role Profile Auditing, and Access Control Auditing.

User Profile Auditing validates data related to user profile attributes, user memberships in groups, user provisioning, user status, etc.

Role Profile Auditing validates data related to role profile attributes, role groups, etc.

Access Control Auditing validates data related to access controls.

Auditing can provide very vital information for IAM system by:

- Validating and logging all the discrepancies in accounts management and role management (like inappropriate accounts creation, role creation, role attestation to users, etc.)
- Validating and logging all the discrepancies in access control (like inappropriate access privileges to users and how they have received)
- Validating and logging all the discrepancies in authentication and authorization

Primary details are needed for auditing are:
Audit name
Audit type
Audit performed on (Date & time)
Audit performed on resources (HR database, AD, etc.)
Target name
Target type
Compliance score %

Analytics and Reporting

Analytics is the process of collecting the data, analyzing the patterns of data, and understanding existing data from IAM repositories or databases and making meaningful decisions.

Reporting is the process of reporting meaningful and useful information in an accessible format to privileged users to make communications and decisions for the stakeholders in an organization.

Analytics and Reporting provides easy to understand information for performance measurement, risk analysis, and mitigation.

Analytics and Reporting consolidates important information on IAM systems like:

- Number of users, groups, roles, etc.
- Users created, deleted, reactivated
- Groups created, deleted and reactivated
- Number of locked-out users
- Number of failed authorizations

Continuous Improvement

Continuous improvement initiative is implemented on all the three stages (Strategy for IAM product development, Design for IAM product development, and Operations for IAM product development). Continuous improvement initiative is triggered when there are:

- New business requirements from customer
- Changes in customer's requirements
- Any failures occurred in the existing identity & access management systems
- Any reduction in the quality of the identity & access management systems
- Any justified feedbacks and recommendations
- Any issues in compliance audits

Objectives
- Improve the complete lifecycle activities in IAM product development.
- Improve efficiency, effectiveness, and performance and minimize the interruption of business.

- To define metrics for various activities (for measuring and evaluating the services).

Best Practices for Continuous Improvement
- Process and technical trainings and awareness programs.
- Management support for improving the services.
- Dedicated team for improvement of the services.
- Maintenance of a knowledge base and lessons log.

Continuous Improvement Methods

Continuous improvement methods that are suggested for IAM product development are:
1. Deming cycle
2. SWOT analysis

Deming Cycle - PDCA (Plan, Do, Check, Act)

Plan: This phase defines a series of activities to understand the importance of improvement initiatives with respect to existing IAM solutions/tools like:
- What are the new improvement initiatives, and who initiated it?
- Can we customize the existing tool, or should we buy another supporting tool?
- How much time would it take for customization and development?
- How much efforts does it require (in terms of human resources)?
- Do we have processes defined for the respective improvements?

Develop: This phase defines the series of actions and activities that are needed to implement the planned improvement like:

- Developing the business, functional, user and non-functional requirements.
- Development of the architecture diagrams, model diagrams, HLD and LLD.
- Preparation of test cases.
- Development of the new features and functionalities.
- Development of the documentation or updating the existing documentation.

Check: This phase defines the control activities to ensure that the developed activities are implemented correctly and assesses the yielded results with the expected results. It involves activities like:

- Testing the delta package and newly developed functionalities.
- Testing the integrated solution with new features and functionalities.
- Conducting performance, load, and stress testing.
- Verification and validation of the documentation.

Act: Reviews the actions performed, identifies effective ways of doing things, and documents the lessons learned. It involves activities like:

- Deployment of the finished solutions.
- Collection of feedback and recommendations.
- Documentation of the lessons learned.

SWOT Analysis

SWOT analysis is another improvement methodology which identifies strengths, weakness, opportunities, and threats of the existing system and defines the proactive and reactive measures for improving the IAM systems.

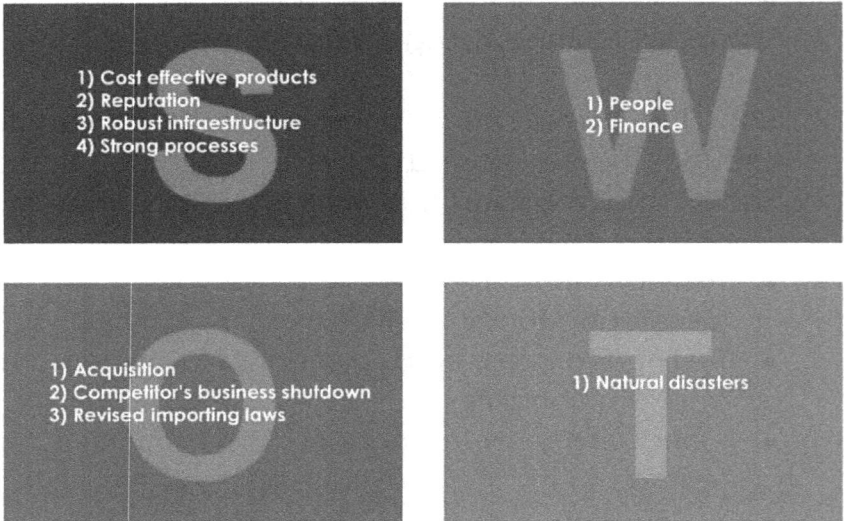

Fig 15: SWOT Analysis

234

Metrics for Identity and Access Management

Some of the key metrics identified for IAM are:
1. Average number of distinct credentials per user.
2. Number of password reset calls per month.
3. Number of account lockouts.
4. Number of new access requests logged in infrastructure.
5. Number of new accounts provisioned using IAM tools.
6. Number of non-expiring information systems (that do not enforce a password expiry policy).
7. Number of ghost/orphan accounts (Ghost/Orphan accounts: Accounts without a user).
8. Number of dormant accounts (accounts which are inactive for at least N days).
9. Number of defined policies.
10. Number of incorrect access granting's.
11. Number of full, partial, and incremental backups.
12. Number of privileged accounts without an owner.
13. User password age (maximum time duration that the password can be operated without a password change).
14. Time taken to fulfill an access request.

235

15. Time taken for provisioning on an access request.
16. Time taken for de-provisioning all services for an employee.
17. Time taken to develop any IAM application.
18. Number of issues and non-compliances found in audits.
19. Percentage of false acceptance rate (FAR) using IAM tools.
20. Percentage of false rejection rate (FRR) using IAM tools.
21. Percentage of false acceptance rate (FAR) using biometric devices.
22. Percentage of false rejection rate (FRR) using biometric devices.
23. Number of human resources working in IAM departments.

CSFs for Identity and Access Management

Some of the CSFs for IAM are:
1. Process and Technical training programs for stakeholders.
2. Streamlined administration on the identities and access control.
3. Aligning user access rights with business responsibilities.
4. Effective identity and access management plans, policies, and procedures.
5. Defined standards (syntax) for user identity naming conventions.
6. Unified policies for all kinds of information systems, web, and applications.
7. Automated workflows for identity and access grants.
8. Ability to determine the status of users at any time, whether if they are working in the organization or terminated from the organization.
9. Thorough understanding of SLAs, SLOs, UCs, OLAs.
10. Thorough implementation of information security policies and standards across the enterprise to mitigate risks.

237

11. Leveraging the existing identity infrastructure (software, technology, hardware, etc.) as much as possible.
12. Usage of widely recognized best practices and standards.
13. Involvement of key stakeholders while making important decisions.
14. Consolidation of access management team contacts list (IT Contacts list should have the summary of responsible people for a specific service, with their name, contact number, email id, and contact time).
15. Maintenance of lessons log and how the previous issues were resolved.
16. Documentation of suggestions and feedbacks for improving the IAM system.

IAM FOR PRACTITIONERS AND EXPERTS

Deep dive into IAM

This section is intended for technical experts, management staff, quality assurance, and auditing professionals for describing the niche knowledge areas in IAM discipline like:
- ✓ IAM Consulting
- ✓ New functionalities in IAM solutions
- ✓ Evolving trends in IAM
- ✓ Technology in IAM
- ✓ Guidelines for IAM tasks
- ✓ Risks in IAM
- ✓ Maturity levels of IAM
- ✓ Best practices for IAM
- ✓ SOX criteria for IAM processes/tools
- ✓ ISO/IEC 27001 requirements for IAM
- ✓ Checklist for IAM product selection
- ✓ Auditing checklist for IT management with respect to IAM
- ✓ Cost and time graph for IAM products implementation

IAM Consulting

IAM consulting for any organizations can be defined into five phases as Analysis, Response, Design, Implementation, and Improvement.

Analysis

Analysis is the phase where IAM consultants, project managers, and business analysts are involved in analyzing the RFP (Request for proposal) and BR (Business Requirements) documents received from the customer. It normally involves:

- Understanding the purpose, objectives, and goals of the identity and access management system.
- Identification and understanding the organization offices, located at different locations (in different countries), and applicable IT laws.
- Identification and understanding of the information systems (databases, applications, directory servers, etc.) involved and platforms (operating systems, virtual machines and etc.).
- Clarify the questions, concerns, and confusions with the customer.
- Identify the risks involved in the project.

Response

In this phase, an IAM consultant takes advice from project managers, business analysts, and solution architects and drafts a response through:

- High level project plan with appropriate project management methodology, schedule, resource estimation, milestones, acceptance criteria, etc.
- Definition of technologies that will be used in the IAM implementation.
- Conditions and constraints.
- Deliverables and acceptance criteria.

Design

In this phase, a project manager takes an active role and starts managing the project very actively; IAM consultants and solution architects design the IAM processes and solutions with respect to business requirements. The design phase is initiated with:

- Consolidation of business requirements, definition of user requirements, and acceptance criteria.
- Preparation of HLD documents and LLD documents.
- Definition of methods for data communication between databases, applications, directories, proxy servers, firewalls, etc.

- Installation of identity management products in IT infrastructure.
- Customization of identity management products as per business and user requirements.
- Testing the identity and access management products/services with dummy data to check functionality, usability, reliability, performance, and security.

Implementation

In this phase, identity and access management products are implemented on specific applications, or IAM services are made accessible for a specific set of users/ administrators to verify and validate functionality, usability, reliability, performance, and security.

Implementation can be done through batch processing/phased approach and big bang approach. But the best practice would be a phased approach where IAM services are implemented on one application at a time or on a specific set of users.

In this phase all details are tracked and logged with respect to IAM products and its interfacing applications through transactions per second, number of users that it can support, etc. After consolidating all the logs, this information would be useful to validate the effectiveness of the IAM products implementation.

243

Improvement

IAM consultants note the problems, risks, issues, concerns, and complaints with respect to the IAM services in a live IT infrastructure, and they implement improvement initiatives (could be better solutions/customization on the existing systems) to improve the identity and access management system.

Scenario on IAM consulting project

Company "A" needs identity management system implemented in an organization.

Currently, IAM tasks are implemented manually by a local IT team which obviously involves the risk of human errors in provisioning processes and consequence of various compliance issues. Hence, an auto-provisioning tool is needed to replace the current human processes thereby minimizing human efforts on security provisioning and thus improving the efficiency and accuracy.

Company "A" has many offices in countries like Egypt, China, Bangladesh, United States of America, England, and Germany.

So, here is the list of business requirements:

- Single identity management system for all users across all countries
- Auto-provisioning and de-provisioning should happen on applications SAP, Peoplesoft, Jive, Salesforce, and Wintel platforms
- Implementation of SSO (Single sign on service)
- Reliable IAM systems

Now here is the list of activities and tasks that should be done by an IAM consultant:

- Analyze the purpose and objectives of the identity and access management system.

  Purpose: Single identity management system for all users across all countries.

  Objectives:

  1. *Auto-provisioning, control, and de-provisioning on applications SAP, Peoplesoft, Jive, Salesforce, Wintel platforms, LDAP, and Web servers.*
  2. *Implementation of SSO (Single sign on service)*
  3. *Maintenance of reliable IAM systems*

- Identify the organization offices, located at different locations (in different countries), and applicable IT laws and standards.

- Identify and understand the information systems (databases, applications, directory servers, etc.) and platforms (operating systems, virtual machines, etc.) compatibility with IAM products.

- Clarify questions, concerns, and confusions with the customer.

- Identify the risks and challenges involved in integrating different information systems with IAM products.

- Definition of mitigation plans for the risks.

- Definition of technologies, tools, conditions, and constraints that will be applicable in the IAM implementation.

- Definition of deliverables.

- Confirmation from the customer with respect to plans on project, quality, deliverables, risks, etc.

- Definition of business requirements.
  BR001: Auto-provisioning to applications SAP, Peoplesoft, Jive, Salesforce, Wintel platforms.
  BR002: Auto-de-provisioning to applications SAP, Peoplesoft, Jive, Salesforce, Wintel platforms.
  BR003: Data synchronization between identity management systems and other data sources.
  BR004: Single sign on implementation.
  BR005: Stable and reliable IAM systems.

- Definition of user requirements.
  UR001: IAM administrators should have all privileges including provisioning and de-provisioning all users on applications SAP, Peoplesoft, Jive, Salesforce, and Wintel platforms.

247

UR002: IS and Quality team members should be able to view the transactions in all IAM solutions. They should only be able to view the data - no edit or delete privileges.

UR003: Other IT administrators (database administrators, directory administrators, application administrators) should have provisioning privileges only with their respective applications and databases.

UR004: Partners should only have read access privileges to their assigned applications and only their profile information.

UR005: Employees should only have access privileges to their assigned applications, profile information, and other profiles.

- Preparation of HLD documents and LLD documents.
  HLD: High level documents should depict the topology of identity management products (interfacing with other databases, directories, and application servers), architecture of identity management products, and how communication happens through its different layers.
  LLD: Low level design documents should comprise customizations made on identity management and access management products.

248

- Conduct a POC (Proof of concept) to check if the systems work as they were planned.

- Installation of identity management products in IT infrastructure.

- Customization of identity management products as per business and user requirements.

- Testing identity and access management products/services with dummy data to check functionality, usability, reliability, performance, and security.

- Testing the IAM products with live data in a phased approach.

- Making a track and log of all issues, errors, and suggestions.

- Improve the products and processes with respect to feedback.

Skill sets required for an IAM Consultant

Skill sets required by IAM consultants can be categorized into three areas: Technical, Process, and General skills.

Technical skills:
- User provisioning technologies like SAML, SPML, XACML, etc.
- Knowledge on enterprise directory/LDAP directory servers
- Knowledge on web services security
- Database administration skills
- Windows server administration skills
- Programming knowledge in technologies like Java, Dotnet, etc.
- Scripting knowledge
- Knowledge on both Linux and Windows environments
- Ability to successfully troubleshoot software systems by following logical and repeatable processes
- Working experience in IAM security products like CA IDM/ Siteminder/ CA Control minder, IBM Tivoli Identity Manager/IBM Tivoli access

Manager, Oracle IDM/Oracle Access Manager, SUN IDM, Novell IDM, or Microsoft FIM

Process skills:
- Knowledge on IT security standards, practices, and recommended considerations.
- Basic knowledge in ITIL/COBIT/MOF processes.
- Basic awareness on ISO/IEC 27000, ISO/IEC 27001, ISO/IEC 27002 standards.
- Basic understanding on risk management.
- Basic understanding of project management methodologies like Agile, Scrum, etc.

General skills:
- Willingness and flexibility to learn new technologies, scale up quickly, and adapt to different roles as the situation demands.
- Ability and willingness to contribute to technical deliverables.
- High customer orientation and quality awareness.
- Excellent verbal and written communication skills.
- High analytical skills.
- Ability to present complex technical topics to both executive and technical personnel in written and verbal form.

Responsibilities of IAM Consultants are:

- Understand ISM core objectives and define technical and business requirements for IAM solutions.
- Design and manage the IAM (Identity & Access Management) solutions.
- Documenting solution architecture and design.
- Installing, configuring, customizing, and implementing IAM products.
- Interacting with customers and team members onshore & off-shore to solve implementation problems.
- Define integration approaches for IAM with external systems.
- Create and maintain an overall design of the complete IAM environment and ecosystem that allows for a comprehensive overview.
- Provide integration and federation solutions for internal and external use.
- Make technical recommendations and define alternative approaches to resolve technical problems.
- Support the development team when issues arise during the software development lifecycle.

Skill sets required for an ISM Consultant

Skill sets required by ISM consultants can be categorized into three areas: Technical, Process, and General skills.

Technical skills:
- Knowledge on system administration, firewall administration, network protocols, routers, hubs, and switches.
- Knowledge on network security and troubleshooting.
- Knowledge on Security Testing and Vulnerability Testing (Nessus, etc.).
- Should hold certifications like CISSP, CISM, CISA, and ISO/IEC27001 LA/LI.
- Should be a certified professional in ethical hacking (CEH).

Process skills:
- Experience with information security management of third-party management suppliers as required under ISO27001.
- Having implemented and maintained deep knowledge of ISO27001 and ISO27002.

- Thorough knowledge on ITIL/COBIT/MOF process development and improvement.
- Good understanding of Identity/Access management process and process activities.
- Good understanding on BCP, BCM, and ITSCM processes.
- Thorough knowledge on risk management methodologies.
- Thorough understanding of project management methodologies like Agile, Scrum, etc.

General skills:
- Ability to present complex technical topics to both executive and technical personnel in written and verbal form.
- Experience in analyzing & resolving technical problems.
- Good reporting and analysis skills.
- Strong customer & service focus.
- Good Interpersonal skills.

Responsibilities of ISM Consultants are:
- Design of the security strategy.
- Security incidents handling and analysis.
- Security and compliance team build up and management.

- Define the information security management processes and keep improving them.
- Preparing formal reports and report presentations to top level management.
- Support technical team as a subject matter expert in networking systems, operating systems, database systems, firewall systems, intrusion detection/prevention systems, remote access systems, threat and vulnerability, forensic technology solutions, etc.
- Understand government security related policies and regulations; design and deploy practices to comply with policies and regulations.

Business logic in Identity Management tools or applications

Scenario: How identity management tools provision accounts to an information system when a user joins an organization.

Pre-requisites:
1) Identity management server should be well integrated with information systems in the IT infrastructure.

Business logic:
1) User joins the organization and submits all relevant information regarding his identity, education, etc.
2) HR collects all data from the user with respect to employee name, date of birth, passport number, educational information, etc.
3) HR saves the entire employee's information in the HR database and creates employee records assigning a manager, department, and a unique individual account name for every employee record.

4) HR database is then synchronized with LDAP directory, so that all the employees' data is stored in directories (in a tree like structure).
5) LDAP directory information is then synchronized with identity management tools or identity management server.
6) Identity management server then creates an account name for the user in identity management server and database.
7) As per the policies and processes defined in identity management server, user accounts are provisioned with their respective information systems.
8) If the identity management server cannot integrate with defined information systems in the IT infrastructure, the user will be informed through his Manager/Supervisor to submit access requests for specific information systems.
9) Accordingly, the identity management administrator verifies approval from the user's managers/supervisors and grants access for the requested information system.

Scenario: How identity management tool de-provisions the user account from an identity management server and information system when a user decides to leave the organization.

Business logic:
1) User submits his resignation to his Manager and HR.
2) HR sets the last working date for the employee in HR database, and the account is disabled with respect to the date.
3) HR database is then synchronized with LDAP directory which also means that the disabled user account's information is sent to the LDAP directory.
4) LDAP directory information is then synchronized with identity management tools or identity management server which also means that the disabled user account's information is sent to identity management server.
5) Once the identity management server is updated with the disabled account information, the respective application access is also disabled.
6) If the identity management server cannot integrate with defined information systems, then the administrator of the identity management

server disables the user account with respect to applications.

Business logic in Access Management tools or applications

Scenario: A user submits a request to access a web resource in an organization which has implemented identity and access management tools.

Business logic:

1) User tries to access a web resource (which means the user sends a request for a web resource through a web browser).

2) Webgate intercepts the requests and checks with the access management server whether the requested web resource is protected or not.

3) If the web resource is not protected, then the user would be able to access the requested resource.

4) If the resource is protected, then access management server will authenticate the user.

5) User enters the login credentials and webgate sends the credentials to the access management server.

6) Access management server verifies and validates the credentials with respect to the backend which is generally a LDAP server.

7) If the user credentials match with the details in LDAP server, it means the user is authenticated.

8) Next, Access management server verifies whether the user credentials is authorized to access the web resource.

9) If the user is authorized, then the access management server will create a session id and it is passed to the webgate.

10) Web gate passes this information to the user (which is user's browser) and the user will be able to access the requested resource.

11) If the user is not authorized, then an error page will be displayed in the browser (as per the defined error message in the access management tool).

Business logic in Authentication and SSO

Scenario: A user logs into an enterprise portal through authentication and will not have to enter the user credentials every time he accesses a web resource.

Primary conditions:
1) Access management servers in all domains must use same policies.

Business Logic:

1) User accesses a web resource by entering the URL in the browser.
2) Webgate intercepts the requests and sends it to access management server.
3) Access management server redirects and asks the user to authenticate.
4) User enters the login credentials and webgate sends the credentials to the access management server.
5) User enters the login credentials.
6) If the login credentials are verified and validated, then the access management server sends the unique identifiers (token and cookies)

which are persistent for some specific time duration (e.g. 1 hour or 2 hours).

7) These unique identifiers (token and cookies) are sent to the user's browser through the webgate and are stored in the browser.

8) User is granted access to the web resource.

9) Now, the user accesses another web resource which is on the same domain.

10) As the unique identifiers (token and cookies) are stored in the browser, the user will be able to access the web resource without entering the login credentials.

Business logic in Multi-domain SSO

Scenario: A user logs into an enterprise portal (Web resource 1), and then he tries to access another portal (Web resource 2) which is hosted on another domain (without re-entering the credentials).

Primary conditions:
1) Access servers in all domains must use same policies.
2) Multi-domain works only with web gates.
3) We should designate one web server with web gate as the "Primary Authentication Server".

Business Logic:

1) User enters the login credentials and is logged into the web resource (*web resource1*) through webgate1.
2) User tries to access a web resource (*web resource2*) which is on other domain.
3) Webgate2, designated for *web resource2*, sends the authentication request to the user's browser in search of a primary authentication server.

4) The request for authentication is redirected from the user's browser to the primary authentication server (*web resource1*).

5) Access server generates a session token with a URL (which contains the SSOcookie).

6) Generated session token with the URL is sent to the requested web resource (*web resource2*).

7) The Web gate (webgate2) for web resource2 sets the token for the other domain and the user gets the resource.

Business logic in Identity Federation

Scenario: A user logs into an information system and accesses various protected resources or applications which are hosted on different domains and belonging to different organizations.

Primary conditions:
1) Defined and agreed identity provider and service provider by all organizations in the federation.

Business Logic:

1) User enters the login credentials and tries to connect to the identity provider.
2) Identity provider authenticates the user, and a session cookie is sent to the user's browser.
3) User tries to access an application residing on the service provider.
4) Identity provider creates a SAML assertion based on the session cookie, then it redirects to the service provider.
5) Service provider receives the SAML assertion, identifies the user's identity information, and

maps the user to a local user account on the destination site.

6) An authorization check is done; if the user credentials are authorized, it redirects the user's browser to the protected resource.

7) If the service provider successfully received and validated the user, it will place its own cookie in the user's browser so the user can now navigate between applications in both domains without additional logins.

Approach for implementing IAM products

Well planned and carefully implemented IAM processes and products would bring:
- Improved control on business, reducing costs, improved TCO (Total cost of ownership), and VFM (Value for money).
- Improved levels of compliance and risk management.
- Improved operational efficiency and stakeholder's experience.
- Improved security and eliminating frauds from stakeholders and external audiences.

Approach for implementing IAM products is explained through seven stages as mentioned below:
- Plan
- Design
- Install
- Configure
- Operate
- Evaluate
- Early life support (ELS)

Plan

A plan is a thought or an idea that has been made in advance. It's going to be the same even here. It's a an idea that has been made in advance before implementing any IAM products; and it's going to involve a sequence of activities like:

- Definition of roles and responsibilities in an envisioned IAM product implementation project.
- Understand the business needs of IAM.
- Understand the defined IS policies.
- Definition of the mission, goals, and objectives.
- Identifying and understanding the existing infrastructure.
- Identifying and acquiring the other hardware and software necessary for IAM product implementation.
- Evaluate the available IAM products with respect to cost, scope, functionality, usability, maintainability, performance, security, scalability, and support.
- Assess the stakeholder's opinions on the list of products identified.
- Identify the risks and issues with respect to the list of IAM products selected, technology integrations, regulations, and stakeholders.

Design

The sequence of activities which defines and frames a logical and acceptable solution with the help of various subcomponents (processes, technologies, architectural diagrams, model diagrams, and documentation), criteria, constraints, boundaries, and interfaces is called as design.

Design phase for IAM products implementation involves activities like:

- Understanding/development of business requirements, functional requirements, user requirements, and non-functional requirements.
- Understanding/definition of the existing IT architecture diagrams and proposed IT architecture diagrams after IAM tools are deployed.
- Understanding/development of IAM tool architecture.
- Defining the local machines, remote machines, virtual machines, coherence servers, and virtual hosting services.
- Understand and identify the dependencies.
- Understanding/definition of the information flow from IAM tools to different databases and repositories and vice-versa.

- Understanding/definition of use case scenarios with respect to different users (employees, contractors, vendors, partners, etc.)
- Understanding/definition of data architecture like table name, field name, label name, form name, data types, etc.
- Defining the rollback contingency plan.

Install

Activity that deploys the IAM tools on the associated hardware or information systems is called installation. Installation phase for IAM product implementation involves activities like:

- Installation of networking devices (routers, firewalls, load balancers, cables, etc.)
- Configuration and installation of servers, clients, operating systems, software platforms, patches, fixes, etc.
- Installation of databases, directories, virtual directories, IAM tools, web servers, web gates, access gates, proxy server, etc.
- Installation of plug-ins for different applications

Configure

Configure is an activity that arranges and organizes the IT artifacts to establish a relationship, make them communicate with each other, modify the default settings of the artifacts, and make them work yielding to a specific goal.

Configuration phase for IAM products implementation involves activities like:

- Setting the IAM environment (production, test, and development).
- Configuration of web servers.
- Creation of schemas in database.
- Configuration of ports, IP addresses for databases, directories, etc.
- Configuration of IAM tools with databases, directories, and applications.
- Verification of synchronization from databases to IAM tools.
- Starting, tuning, administering, managing, and stopping the servers.
- Customizing the workflows.
- UI customization and form customization.
- Reconciliation of the identity information from HR databases to IAM tools.
- Data migration from HR databases to LDAP directories confirming that the synchronization is happening as planned.

Operate

Operate phase showcases the actual results/values delivered by the implemented IAM products.
Operate phase for IAM products implementation involves activities like:

- Administration of the IAM tools, web servers, directories, databases, etc.
- Provisioning and de-provisioning identities, identity governance, access provisioning and control, access certification and re-certification, entitlements management, auditing, etc.
- Administration of users, passwords, roles, rules, entitlements, policies, etc.
- Data importing and exporting

Evaluate

Verification and validation of the implemented IAM product is the main objective of evaluation. The evaluation phase for IAM product implementation involves:

- Functional testing
- Performance testing
- Security testing
- General testing (nonfunctional requirements)

Early life support

Early life support is the initial support provided by a team when there is new or changed IT services in an IT organization. ELS phase for IAM product implementation involves:

- Providing on-call support or technician's support for operational activities mentioned in the operate phase.
- Providing support for any unknown issues that have occurred after deploying IAM tools and making a log of all the issues.
- Preparation of documentation like SOP's (Standard Operating Procedures), knowledge base, user manuals, and other collaterals for performing different tasks.

New functionalities in IAM solutions

Self-registration

Self-registration is a functionality which provides the ability to create user accounts by the end-users as per defined policies, procedures, and guidelines.

After creation of user accounts, it will be checked and approved by the system administrator. Self-registration would help the users to get onboard at work quickly and cost effectively.

Advantages of self-registration

- Takes less time in provision of user accounts
- Saves effort and additional resources for creation of accounts

Disadvantages of self-registration

- It gets complicated, requires more effort, and takes more time, if the user accounts are not created as per defined policies and guidelines

Self-service

Self-Service is the portal that will enable the users of an organization to manage certain services by themselves without any bureaucratic procedures. Self-service helps users to update, manage their personal information, recover the forgotten passwords, manage security token related services, and manage the login access for temporary visitors. Self-service is the feature that can accommodate all the low cost, low risk, and very frequent issues.

Advantages of self-service
- Enables users to gain access to a system by obtaining a new password without requiring assistance from the help desk.
- Reduces help desk costs and time on routine and frequent password reset calls and requests - which is one of the most common types of help desk calls.
- Users can do it themselves without relying on others which wastes time

Single Sign on

Single Sign on (SSO) is a way of managing user access control with same user name and password on various independent software applications, databases, tools, or services. A perfect SSO implementation in an organization's environment will give great relief to users, as they will not have to log in again and again on every application or tool or database or service. Advantages of SSO

- Saves time for users and avoids entering the password again and again.
- Enables the provision of single user name and password for all applications and services.
- Users wouldn't have to remember numerous user id's and passwords.

SSO can be implemented in different approaches as: Web SSO, Federated SSO, and Operating system integrated SSO.

Web SSO

Web SSO enables the users with Single Sign On (SSO) on web applications or web resources. Web SSO is implemented through IAM processes and technologies which consists of web servers, webgates, directories, identity servers, and access servers which then manages user identities, authentication, and authorization.

When a user tries to access a web resource enabled with WebSSO, users are redirected to login with user credentials. If the user is successfully authenticated, HTTP cookies are issued and used by web applications to validate authenticated user sessions.

Federated SSO

Federated SSO enables the users with Single Sign On (SSO) in a federation to access web resources. Federated SSO is implemented through IAM processes and technologies which works with identity provider, service provider, and trusted parties.

277

In federated SSO, the authentication is done by a trusted party, and the users wouldn't be prompted again and again when accessing federated resources.

Enterprise SSO
Enterprise SSO enables the organizational users with Single Sign On (SSO) for all enterprise applications including windows applications. Enterprise SSO can be implemented only when the user accounts are stored in LDAP or Active directory.

Operating system integrated SSO
Operating system integrated SSO enables the users with Single Sign On (SSO) to all the interfacing and integrated information systems with the operating system.

Reconciliation

Reconciliation is the activity which synchronizes the data or information from an IAM object to another object (For example: data synchronization from a HR database to an IAM application).

IAM solutions implement reconciliation in two different ways: one as trusted reconciliation and the other as target reconciliation.

Trusted reconciliation is the reconciliation of data from

a trusted database to an IAM product. Here, the term trusted is used because the database is treated as a source of trusted or reliable information.

Target reconciliation is the reconciliation of data from an IAM product to a database. Here, the term target is used because the database is treated as a target and data or information is synchronized from an IAM product.

The above two ways of reconciliation can be performed in two different approaches as full reconciliation and incremental reconciliation.

Attestation

Attestation is an activity or task in identity management which bears evidence that a designated role (like a manager or administrator) has verified and approved that a specific transaction (user's entitlements, user's privileges, user's) is being performed with accuracy, integrity, and compliance.

Attestation should be carried out on a regular basis to have effective control on user accounts privileges, entitlements, etc.

Evolving trends in IAM

Identity Federation

Identity Federation is the subset of identity management process which manages the user identities of different enterprises involving partners, customers, suppliers, etc. in a federated approach with the help of common policies and protocols. Identity federation enables users in accessing different enterprise networks and shares secure information exchange without requiring many passwords.

Identity federation is the concept which breaks the boundaries and complexities involved in enterprise communications without using numerous protocols, VPN's (Virtual Private Networks), and other networking devices.

Benefits of identity federation:
- Defines the procedure for multi-enterprise access and authentication without any risks.
- Improves business relationships with various enterprises involving partners, customers, suppliers, etc.
- Establishes secure connections and provides accessibility on valuable information systems which are owned by 3rd party organizations.

- Reduces the costs of integration between different information systems.

Identity Governance

Identity Governance is the subset of identity management process which determines and controls user identities, user access, and the identity information and how they are used, stored, and communicated.

Benefits of identity governance:
- Provides insight into critical access and identity information across the enterprise.
- Develops a proactive mitigation and resolution plan for identity and access challenges.
- Minimizes the risks of non-compliances and failures in audits.
- Improves organizational efficiency with respect to the administration and management of user identities.
- Develops automated tasks for manual routine work like on-boarding, change of roles, termination of employees, etc.

Identity Analytics

Identity analytics is the subset of identity management process which analyzes, identifies meaningful information on user identities, access controls and policies - enabling administrators to make intuitive and better decisions.

Benefits of Identity Analytics:
- Captures all user identity information in detail "why and how" about all transactions in user identities, access controls, etc.
- Manages and mitigates risks and issues proactively and reactively.
- Performs periodic reviews on all identity management process, policies, and data.
- Helps in achieving compliance.

Privileged Identity Management

Privileged Identity Management (PIM) is the subset of identity management process which administers, controls, and manages privileged accounts (like administrator, super user) and their activities. It is an explicit process defining the procedures for provisioning, control, tracking and de-provisioning of privileged identities.

Because of increasing internal attacks, especially from the super users and administrators, organizations are in great need of PIM.

Benefits of privileged identity management:
- Provides better security for privileged accounts and improves compliance and efficiency.
- Increased administrator's productivity without exposing the administrator's accounts to issues like unlocking, disabling, etc.
- Meticulous and consistent watch on privileged accounts and their access.
- Reduces the risks in data confidentiality, integrity, and loss from privileged accounts.

Why do we need PIM?
- Manually keeping a track of all privileged accounts in a world class conglomerate is near impossible.
- To discover the privileged accounts automatically in applications, databases, directories, etc.
- Tracking and updating passwords of privileged accounts at regular intervals as per defined policies.
- To audit and report access on the privileged accounts ensuring compliance.

Access control based on devices

Access control based on devices is a new concept in IAM where the access to specific information systems is controlled based on the type of device, location of the device, network of the device, etc.

With the new and uprising trends, BYOD (Bring your own device) and WFH (Work from home) options in IT industry, access control based on devices has come into great focus playing an important role in identity and access management.

Access control through devices is done after assessing the factors like:

- Is this company owned asset or employee owned device?
- Is the device on a private or public network?
- Is the device a single user or multi-user device?
- Is the device encrypted?

Biometrics in IAM

IAM experts predict that the use of biometric technology would proliferate in the next few years because of the increasing demand in security (confidentiality, integrity, and non-repudiation) - especially for sensitive information in industries like financial, PCIDSS (Payment Card Industry Data

Security Standard), defense/military, immigration, health care, home security, government, etc.

Not only for information systems, it would also bring good benefits for users eliminating the very frequent issues like forgetting a password, password hacking, password changes, account lockouts, etc.

Biometric authentication is an evolving technique where unique physical characteristics (finger prints, facial features, iris patterns in the eyes, voice recognition) of users are verified, validated, and then provided with access to the respective resources.

A biometric device scans the biometric data of the users, uses software to convert the data into digital information, and verifies the data with the stored data in the backend (LDAP).

Examples: Fingerprint scanners, Voice recognition systems, Face recognition systems, Iris and retinal scans, etc.

Important factors which evaluate the effectiveness of biometric devices are accuracy, number of verifications/minute, false acceptance rate, false rejection rate, CER (Crossover Error Rate), reliability, availability, and ability to detect counterfeiting.

IAM in Cloud Computing

With the increasing demand in cloud computing and its innovative services (SaaS, IaaS, PaaS, etc.) many organizations are adapting themselves to cloud technology. IAM plays a very important role in cloud computing; any ignorance on confidentiality, integrity, and privacy would lead to complete collapse of cloud services and cloud infrastructure.

Any loosely developed identity and access management implementations on a cloud can lead to severe risks like loss of data, loss of reputation, and severe penalizations.

Effective IAM processes and tools can give great advantage for the CSP (Cloud Service Provider) and the cloud infrastructure by strengthening security aspects (confidentiality, integrity, and privacy) and eliminating manual, redundant tasks like creation, control, and management of numerous user accounts and passwords.

IAM provides numerous benefits to cloud models (public, private, community, and hybrid) and services (IaaS, PaaS, SaaS, etc.) with:

- Agile, accurate provisioning and de-provisioning of IT accounts

  As cloud services main objective is on demand service provision; hence, provisioning and de-provisioning access to cloud services and resources should be very prompt and precise. Good IAM tools with workflows enables tool administrators to provide and deactivate access to resources and services promptly and precisely without any discrepancies.

- SSO (Single Sign-on Service)
  Numerous applications credentials in a service/services (SaaS, IaaS, PaaS, etc.) would make the user's life frustrating; hence, SSO can provide great value to cloud computing infrastructure. SSO enables great usability as users would only have to sign in once and gain access to all resource/services in a specific cloud service.

- Meticulous control
  Users in cloud have access to many resources and services, and it's very important to know 'who has access to what', 'where they are accessing it', and 'what they are doing'. IAM tools can provide central visibility and control on all cloud infrastructures.

- Precise management of access privileges
  Today, clouds have evolved in numerous models (private, public, community, hybrid, etc.), and

287

managing all the users access meticulously is done through different access controlling methods defined in IAM like: Role based access control, Policy based access control, Discretionary access control, etc.

Identity Relationship Management

Traditionally, Identity and access management was viewed and perceived as a process which had strict demarcations to only a specific organization; IAM was used only for organizational stakeholders to protect organizational data.
But now organizations have a desperate need to engage with different stakeholders (partners, suppliers, customers, contractors, etc.), for better communication, transparency, trust, and better relationships; that is the focus of IRM (Identity Relationship Management).

Identity relationship management is a new approach redefined for Identity and Access Management. It defines a standardized approach for managing identities and access privileges for all internal and external stakeholder organization's interactions with current and future customers and with respect to IAM.

What's new in IRM?
Scalability: It can manage any number of users which can be very helpful in cloud computing - unlike other traditional IAM tools.
Interoperability: It can support various technologies and platforms.
Adaptability: It can support a variety of devices like

289

computers, smart phones, gadgets, etc.

Difference between IRM and IAM

IRM	IAM
Focused on extending enterprise reach securely to enable more revenue driving relationships.	Focused on security and protection of who has access to organizational assets.
IRM is about managing identities and access privileges of internal employees and external stakeholders, and it also supports any computing devices.	IAM is about managing the organization's user's identities and access privileges.
Has a broad scope for analysis on current and future customers to discover new business opportunities.	IAM can have an additional task called Identity Analytics to understand the patterns of user identities and their access privileges.

Technology in IAM

This section describes the technological aspects of IAM highlighting what, why, and how (implementation steps) on:

- LDAP
- Directory
- Directory service
- LDAP server
- Virtual directories
- Data synchronization

LDAP

LDAP (Lightweight directory access protocol) is an open standard network protocol occupying a niche position in directory services. It makes itself compatible with any operating system (platform independent) and supports authentication modes through smart cards and biometric devices.

LDAP is a standard for directories to access user account information (which is stored in a tree like structure and grouping network users) like contact details, login information, password, permissions, etc.

Directory

Directory is a repository which stores and manages information of the user identities like name, employee number, email id, contact number, access privileges, etc. It can also store information about assets, business processes, etc. It enables user accounts to provide easily identifiable naming syntax and structure and easily accessible information. It encompasses all its relationship between other user identities, groups, and other objects in an information system.

Directory service

Directory service is a collection of procedures and technologies involved in storing information about users/groups and assets/objects in an organization. Directory services have the following characteristics:

- They are generally used for reading data
- They have enhanced search capabilities
- It has a hierarchical naming structure

Directory services has gained great popularity and demand from its customers in such a way that all IT conglomerates have their own directory services like:

IBM	IBM Tivoli directory server
CA	CA directory
Microsoft	Active directory

Novell	Novell eDirectory
Oracle	OID (Oracle Internet Directory), OUD (Oracle Unified Directory), ODSEE (Oracle Directory Server Enterprise Edition),OVD (Oracle Virtual Directory)

Directory server

Directory server is a server that can add, change, delete, and store user's identity information like names, attributes, credentials, roles, groups, and policies (e.g. user name, email address, user id, password, etc.) in a tree like structure (normally in an alphabetical order) at a specific physical location. It acts as a central repository for storing and managing information in directories.

Virtual directory

Virtual directory is a single, abstract view of the information from enterprise directory servers; it acts as SPOC aggregating identity data in IAM environment especially when there are multiple data sources.
Virtual directories play a very important role in companies where data is scattered across multiple

293

databases, directories, and various information systems. It provides a unified virtual view on data from multiple data sources spread across multiple locations without synchronizing or moving data from its native locations.

LDAP server

LDAP server is a directory server which stores data in directories (in a tree like structure) and uses LDAP protocol as a standard of communication between different directories.

LDAP servers are easy for maintenance and accessibility; it has many other advantages like:

- Easy data modeling
- Servers are lightweight
- Tuning is a snap
- Footprint is small
- Control through command line tools
- Integrated graphical tools availability
- Importing and exporting data is easy
- Optimized for rapid search and retrieval
- Effective security and supports PKI
- Supports multiple languages

LDAP server can be categorized into two types as Master LDAP and Slave LDAP.

Master LDAP: It is the primary repository where administrators are enabled with CRUD privileges (can do modifications on its data); this repository would be accessible by administrators. The main responsibility of master LDAP is to synchronize its data to the Slave LDAP.

Slave LDAP: It is the repository which holds the replicated data from Master LDAP, and it is accessed by various IAM tools. Data in this repository cannot be modified as here the data is read-only. The main responsibility of slave LDAP is to provide HA (High Availability) configuration.

Guidelines for IAM tasks

User identity creation

1. User identity should be short and unique (should be unique globally).
2. User identity should be user friendly and easily recallable.
3. User identities should refer the user name or combination of first name, middle name, and last name or should refer to his unique employee identity number.
4. User identity should not spell out some vulgar or bad word.
5. A user identity should never be reused again by another employee.
6. User identity should never refer to the user's position or date of birth.
7. It would be better to assign permissions and privileges to a group/role rather than assigning permissions and privileges explicitly to users.
8. Assignment of owners to all the groups created.

User identity de-provisioning

1. If you have to just disable the user account without deleting, make sure you also hide the user account in the directory.
2. Disable/delete user access privileges and permissions before deleting a user from the directory.
3. Set up an auto-reply to the user account's email id stating the employee has resigned and also provide the alternative contact's email id.

Password maintenance

1. Passwords should be a minimum of eight alpha-numeric characters.
2. All passwords should be forcibly changed after every month.
3. Passwords shouldn't be weak or predictable like welcome123, 12345, month name, etc.
4. Passwords shouldn't contain user's first, last, middle name of the employees.

5. Passwords shouldn't be the same as the user id.
6. Passwords should never be shared with anyone else.
7. Passwords should never be written on any posters or notepads.
8. Passwords should never be sent on emails or voice.
9. Enforce change of password after first login.
10. Enforce that the new passwords shouldn't match with the last five passwords used.
11. End users should be aware of the above mentioned information as password policies.
12. All user passwords should be encrypted, hashed, and stored in the database.

User identity reconciliation

1. Perform reconciliation from trusted resources only after getting the approvals from the respective administrators.
2. Do not perform reconciliations consecutively; leave sometime between reconciliations.

3. Reconciliation should be done only when the trusted database and target database has a similar schema structure.

Common mistakes in IAM

Implementation of IAM processes and products is very necessary and critical for every organization, yet organizational management and operational teams cannot rush on making decisions as that would lead to fiascos. Here are some common mistakes that are usually seen in IAM projects:

- Assuming IAM tools are good enough without defining the processes.
- Inappropriate understanding of the existing infrastructure and business processes.
- No definition of cushion time while implementing IAM solutions.
- Inappropriate understanding of the business requirements.
- Inappropriate understanding on information security policies and processes.
- Suspension or de-provisioning of user accounts and user access privileges at incorrect time.
- Inappropriate or inadequate review mechanisms scheduled on user access privileges.
- Reconciliation of data from inappropriate databases.

- Inappropriate availability, capacity, and continuity designs for IAM solutions.
- Inadequate testing (functionality, security, usability, scalability, integration, and failover) on deployed products.
- Inadequate awareness training about information security.
- Complex security measures creates new problems.
- Insufficient documentation or inadequate knowledge transfer for operational teams.
- Inappropriate understanding on cookies and cookie management would make the IAM system vulnerable to numerous attacks.
- Ignoring or inappropriate implementation of firewalls, proxy servers, load balancers, and webgates.
- Inappropriate data migration between databases or data migration from database to IAM tools or vice-versa.
- Ignoring the importance of a demilitarized zone.
- Easy going on the security measures for internal stakeholders and employees.

Maturity levels for IAM

Maturity levels for Identity and Access Management can be defined using five stages as Initial, Repeatable, Defined, Managed, and Optimized.

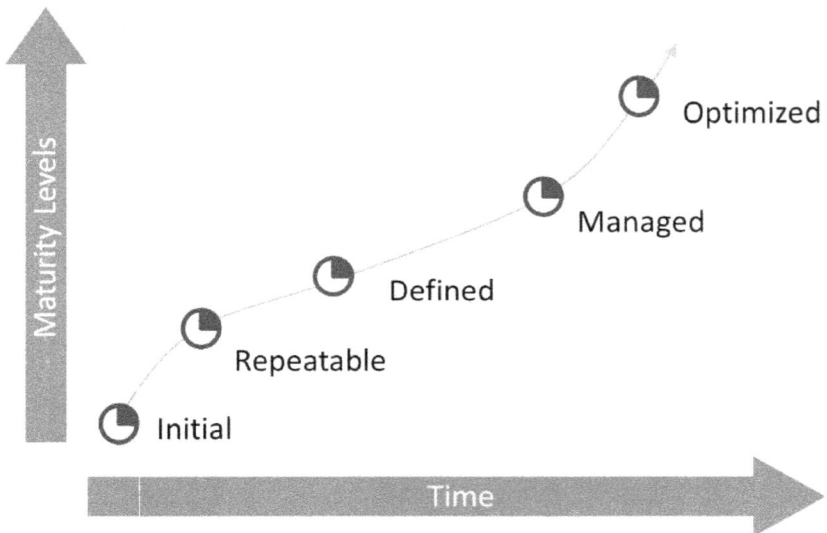

Fig 16: Maturity Levels for IAM

Initial
In this stage, an organization's IAM characteristics would be:
- Manual identity creation, provisioning, and de-provisioning

- Helpdesk agents do the password resets and account unlocking
- No identity reviews are performed

Repeatable

In this stage, an organization's IAM characteristics would be:

- Defined processes and policies for managing all identities
- Directory integration and synchronization with other applications
- Automated identity provisioning and de-provisioning
- Automated/manual reviews on identities at regular intervals

Defined

In this stage, an organization's IAM characteristics would be:

- Password resets and account lockouts performed through self-service portals
- Defined strong authentication
- Defined roles for managing the identities
- Reviews on access certification and recertification
- Defined access controlling mechanisms

Managed

In this stage, an organization's IAM characteristics would be:

- Centralized view of all identities at all points of time.
- Single user identity and password for accessing all information systems.
- Defined identity governance system.
- Defined federated system for all user identities of partners, customers, users, and others.

Optimized

In this stage, an organization's IAM characteristics would be:

- Multi-factored authentication
- Fine grained RBAC
- Automated notifications about the IAM tasks
- Analytics and Reporting done on all identity information
- Regular audits performed
- Defined identity analytics

Best practices for IAM

1. Implementation of IAM should not start with tool implementation; instead, it should start with definition of IAM processes understanding vision, business drivers, and goals.
2. Involvement of the all key stakeholders (HR and IT teams) in the project implementation right from the beginning.
3. Understand and address the concerns of application owners, administrators, and other key stakeholders.
4. Select and purchase the IAM tools - only after PoC (Proof of Concept) and written documentation mentioning what is out of the box and what needs customization.
5. Definition of IAM processes should be done by referring to ITIL, MOF, and COBIT best practices.
6. Leverage existing identity infrastructure.
7. Create links between IT roles and business roles.
8. Select a solution which is scalable, easy for maintenance, and integrates with applications.
9. Create unique identifications for login identities, employee numbers, and email addresses.
10. Define access controls using RBAC, PBAC, ABAC, etc.

11. Automate identity administration tasks like provisioning, de-provisioning, reconciliation, password reset, access controls, audits at regular intervals, etc.
12. Conduct appropriate risk analysis before deployment of any major tasks.
13. Regularly test the IAM systems and processes.
14. Deploy IAM solutions on applications and users in a phased approach one after the other.
15. Fully backup IAM objects (with data) at regular intervals.
16. Perform a post implementation review after IAM implementation in the infrastructure.
17. Adhere to IS (Information Security) policies in IT operational activities.
18. Conduct internal audits with specifications and code of practices as defined in ISO/IEC27001 and ISO/IEC27002.
19. Never set vendor-supplied default passwords as a baseline for the implemented IAM products.
20. Protect all IAM systems against malware and regularly update anti-virus software.

SOX Criteria for IAM Process/Tools

1. Do procedures exist and are they followed to authenticate all users of the system to support the validity of transactions?

2. Do procedures exist and are they followed to maintain the effectiveness of authentication and access mechanisms (e.g. regular password changes)?

3. Do procedures exist and are they followed to ensure timely action relating to requesting, establishing, issuing, and suspending user accounts?

4. Does a control process exists and is it followed to periodically review and confirm access rights?

5. Do you have appropriate controls to ensure that neither party can deny transactions and that controls are implemented to provide transaction initiation and approval?

ISO/IEC27001 and 27002 Requirements for IAM

1. Do you have a defined IS policy?

2. Do you conduct periodic reviews on IS policies?

3. Do you have defined roles and responsibilities for managing identity and access management?

4. Do you have a defined access control policy?

5. Do you have a defined user account creation policy?

6. Do you have a defined policy for removal of access rights?

7. Do you have a defined policy for user account deletion?

8. Do you have defined user password management policies (Password usage, Password reset, Password lockout, etc.)?

9. Do you have a defined policy for review of user access rights?

10. Do you have a defined policy for privileged accounts management?

11. Do you have a defined policy for secure log-on procedures?

12. Do you have the session time-out method implemented in your information systems?

13. Do you have defined policies for all changes on user identities, entitlements, roles, etc.?

14. Do you have information security awareness, education, and training programs conducted?

Checklist for Identity Management Product Selection

Today there are many companies providing numerous identity management solutions; hence, here is a checklist which tries to help organizations and IT management to evaluate the available identity management solutions.

1. Does the solution create, update, and delete user accounts?

2. Is the solution available to administrators from any web browser?

3. Is the solution designed to support users both internal stakeholders and external stakeholders (like partners, suppliers, and contractors) in the enterprise?

4. Does the solution leverage existing infrastructure (emails and browsers) to facilitate automated approvals for account creation?

5. Does the solution provide the flexibility to map your existing business processes?

6. Does the solution allow delegation of approval authority to another approver (or multiple approvers)?

7. Can the solution communicate information to other applications or data stores?

8. Can the product support rule-based routing for approvals?

9. Does the solution require automated approvals for changing account values?

10. Does the product support customization?

11. Can status changes in user accounts (e.g. job promotion captured in HR system) automatically drive changes in user access privileges?

12. Can the solution completely and automatically delete all access privileges on the day of departure or the next day of departure?

13. Will the solution detect and track manual changes made on user accounts?

14. When the changes are detected, can the solution alert/notify designated personnel?

15. Can the solution be used to enforce privacy policy?

16. Does the solution support role-based access control?

17. Does the solution support assignment of users to multiple roles?

18. Does the solution support assignment of users to hierarchical or inherited roles?

19. Does the solution provide the ability to specify exclusionary roles that prevent certain roles from being assigned a conflicting role?

20. Does the solution allow roles to be defined at any time or not at all (rather than requiring role definitions prior to implementation)?

21. Can the solution assign users individual access rights in addition to a role?

22. Does the solution dynamically and automatically change access rights based on changes in user roles?

23. Can the solution generate unique IDs consistent with cooperative policies?

24. Is the solution easy to use for both end users and administrators?

25. Is the solution highly scalable to adapt to growth in users, applications, and access methods?

26. Does the solution work securely over WANs across firewalls?

27. Does the solution provide an interface to third-party workflow management applications?

28. Does the solution allow resource groups (such as WINDOWS NT group) to be created from the interface?

29. Does the product provide directory management capabilities (specifically the ability to create, update, and delete organizational units and directory groups)?

30. Does the product work with all the leading database servers and application servers?

31. Does the solution include support for open standards?

32. Does the solution offer a rich array of application programming interface - with support for Java, C, C++, dot net, etc.?

Checklist for Access Management Products

Also, there are many companies providing numerous access management solutions; hence, here is a checklist which tries to help organizations and IT management to evaluate the available access management solutions.

1. Can you easily and quickly find a user (or a group of users) and view their access privileges?

2. Does the solution allow you to instantly revoke all of a user's access privileges?

3. Does the solution include support for open standards (SAML, and etc.)?

4. Does the product offer support for all required authentication schemes like X.509 digital certificates, RSA SecureID, etc.?

5. Does the solution implement the open-standard Java Authentication and Authorization Service (JAAS) frameworks to allow any JAAS-compliant

authentication mode to be simply plugged in; does it allow customers a standards-based means to easily develop their own?

6. Does the solution offer the customer a choice in protection of an enterprise's applications and information assets through a broad suite of policy control agents as well as proxy approach?

7. Can the product challenge authenticated users to present a stronger credential (i.e. X.509Certificate) when they attempt to access more sensitive resources?

8. Can the product disable a user account after a configurable number of authentication failure events?

9. Does the product support single sign-on across security domains?

10. Does the product provide centralized security policy enforcement of user entitlements by leveraging role and rule based access control?

11. Does the product allow constraining access based on time (day, date range, time of day), location

(IP range), and strength of authentication level (password vs.X.509 certificate, etc.)?

12. Does the product allow external data to be evaluated dynamically at run-time for policy enforcement?

13. Does the product allow creation of custom policy conditions to determine user authorization?

14. Does the product support the ability for user session to time-out after a configurable amount of time? Are time-outs based on the amount of time a user has been idle?

15. Does the product allow administration of access control policy to be delegated to those that own responsibility for management of the protected application?

16. Does the solution allow enterprise applications and platforms to integrate into the centralized authentication/authorization framework seamlessly?

17. Does the solution offer a rich array of application programming interface - with support for Java, C, C++, Dot net and etc.?

18. Does the product provide high availability and failover capabilities to eliminate any single point of failure?

19. Can the solution be load balanced for high availability using standard, off-the-shelf hardware?

20. Does the product scale linearly as additional hardware is employed?

21. Can the solution perform and scale to meet extranet and internet environments with user populations in the tens or hundreds of millions?

22. Does the product provide up-to-the-minute auditing of all authentication attempts, authorizations, and changes made to access activity and privileges?

Auditing checklist for IT management with respect to IAM

Auditing is a mandatory requirement, protocol, and standard that has to be followed for every business; here is an auditing checklist for IT management with respect to IAM:

1. Is there an IAM strategy defined in the organization?
2. If yes, who has defined it and who is managing it? How often is it updated?
3. Based on what best practices and standards, has the strategy been defined?
4. Do you have documentation with respect to IAM strategy? Is it available to all the organizational stakeholders?
5. Do you identify all regulatory requirements needed with respect to your business?
6. How does your organization get to know about the regulatory requirements that it has to follow?
7. Is the IAM strategy centralized or distributed with respect to geographical locations?
8. Do you know the technologies that are being used in your IAM infrastructure?

9. Do you have clearly defined processes and terminology for risk management?

10. Do you have defined roles and responsibilities for risk management?

11. How often do you conduct risk assessments on the IAM processes and tools deployed?

12. How are risks, threats, and vulnerabilities identified?

13. Do you have policies and guidelines for all IAM operational activities?

14. Are the policies and procedures communicated to the designated individuals of the organization?

15. How often does the organization review user identities and access granted? If there is a continuous review performed by tools, what is the criterion defined in the tools?

16. Do you have defined policies and reviews on non-person accounts, to ensure who has access, who knows the password, and what tasks does the account perform?

17. Do you have distinguished procedures for management of privileged user accounts?

18. What authentication and authorization controls are defined to prevent any misuse? And how are the controls measured?

19. How do you synchronize the data? If you have any tools for synchronization, what is the process,

criteria, conditions and methods for synchronization?

Due diligence for IAM projects

Due diligence in IT operations is an activity which conducts an investigation into operations; it ensures that you have access to all important information about the IT operations that you are going to manage. It enables you to assess the contracts, intellectual property, current operations, risks, issues, legal and regulatory compliance associated.

Due diligence questions for identity and access management can be mentioned as:

Due diligence questions for identity and access management can be mentioned as:

- What are the customer pain points with respect to identity and access management?

- What is the scope of services for identity and access management operations (like privileged access management, federation services, identity analytics, role management, entitlement management, etc.)?

- Are there any internal/external suppliers involved in supporting the identity and access management operations?

- Is there a defined SLA for identity management operations like provisioning and de-provisioning?

- What all regions do you support with respect to identity and access management operations?

- Do you have defined identity and access management process and policies?

- What are the KPIs and metrics defined for identity and access management operations?

- What is the number of existing user accounts and what will it be in future?

- What are the different roles defined in your existing IAM tools?

- Do you need self-help password management option?

- Do you need single sign on (SSO) option in your tools?

- Do you need remote sign on option in your tools?

- Do you need password synchronization option in your tools?

- Do you need multi-factor authentication enabled in your tools?

- What kind of access controls (DAC, MAC, ABAC, RBAC, PBAC, etc.) do you have currently? What do you need?

- Do you have reconciliation functionality in your tools? Do you need reconciliation to happen automatically or manually?

- What are the different data repositories existing in the IT environment?

- Does your identity and access management staff follow the process and policies? Or is there any resistance?

- What is the current staff allocated for identity and access management?

- Is there a defined organizational chart and roles and responsibilities defined?

- What are the different tools used for identity and access management?

- Is the team well trained on tools?

- What is the reason for outsourcing identity and access management operations?

- Have you ever outsourced the operations before? What were the issues you had with your previous supplier?

Quality assessment on IAM projects

Assessment checklist for IAM process and operations will be helpful for IAM process and operational staff to understand how effectively the process has been defined and how the operations are doing. This checklist can also be used by a quality team to evaluate the effectiveness of process and operations. This assessment checklist can be described as below:

- Do you have an access management process defined?

- Are the scope and objectives of the process clearly defined?

- Do you follow the defined process?

- Are those performing the process aware of how to do so?

- Is everyone in the team trained on identity and access process management activities?

- Does the process have a continual service improvement program by which deficiencies in the process are identified and improvements implemented?

- Do you check if approvals are there in place before granting / modifying / revoking access?

325

- Do you monitor and report the access privileges of users to identify & revoke any aberrations/ unauthorized access?

- Do you check with the IT Security Manager/ relevant customer SPOC in case of any clarifications?

- Do you have a copy of the intended access privileges of all in the organization?

- Do you constantly monitor for inactive accounts, orphaned accounts, etc.?

- Do you report deviations to the customer / stakeholder?

- Do you disable the user account on the last working day, when an employee is resigning?

- Do you check if leavers' privileges/ IDs are active and initiate actions to deactivate the same?

- Do you generate access management reports as agreed in SLA?

Cost and Time Graph for IAM products implementation

IAM products implementation in any organization is not a simple task, like any technological product; as IAM products touch base with all information systems and repositories. Generally, implementation of IAM products would always involve integration with active directory controllers, email systems, application server, database servers, directory servers, and various technologies.

Hence, IAM product implementation would obviously involve great costs and complexity till the products are well implemented in the infrastructure. However, after a period of time, IAM products will bring great benefits in terms of:

- Improved Security

  Reduce the risk of internal and external attacks using different security methods like authentication, authorization, etc.

- End user and stakeholders satisfaction

  Better access of information to partners, employees, and customers thus leading to increased productivity, satisfaction, and revenue.

- Reduction of operational costs

  Reduces adding staff in security administration and helpdesk for routine tasks like account lockouts, password resets, updates on profile information, etc.

- Single point of contact for identity and access
Provides centralized information for all identity, access, and compliance issues.
- Organizational maturity
Improves business agility during mergers and acquisitions.

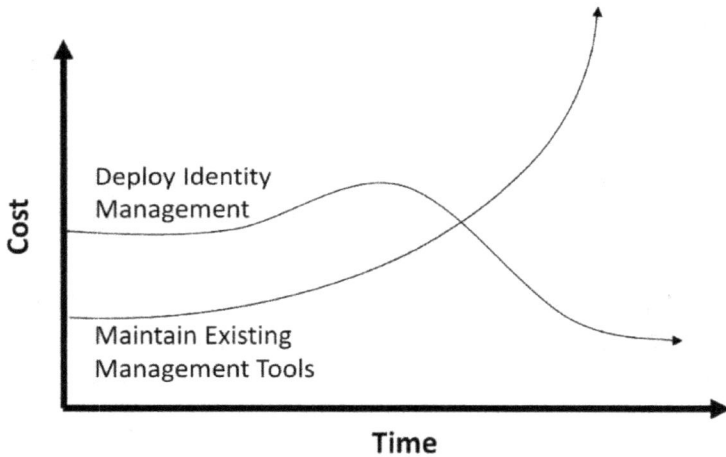

Fig 17: Cost and Time graph for IAM products implementation

328

OVERVIEW OF FEW IAM SOLUTIONS

Oracle Solutions

Oracle identity and access management products allows enterprises to manage and automate the end-to-end lifecycle of user identities, and provides users with secure, fine-grained access to enterprise resources and assets.

Oracle identity and access management products can be grouped into three broad categories as:

- Directory Services
- Access Management
- Identity Management

Directory Services

Directory services, based on the Lightweight Directory Access Protocol (LDAP) are central to an identity and access management strategy. Oracle provides scalable directory and integration technology that meets the requirements of general enterprise deployment, and is also leveraged by other Oracle products in the stack. Oracle Directory Services includes the following components:

Oracle Internet Directory: Oracle Internet Directory is a scalable, robust LDAP v3 - compliant directory service that leverages the scalability, high availability and security features of the Oracle Database. Oracle Internet Directory can serve as the central user repository for identity and access management deployment, simplifying user administration in the Oracle application environment.

Oracle Virtual Directory: Oracle Virtual Directory provides a single, dynamic access point to these data sources through LDAP or XML protocols. It does this by providing a real-time data join and an abstraction layer that exposes a single logical directory, without the need to synchronize or move data from its native location.

Oracle Directory Integration Platform: Oracle Directory Integration Platform is a component of Oracle Internet Directory designed to perform directory synchronization and application integration across various directories and compatible Oracle products. Oracle Directory Integration Platform is also used to implement a corporate meta-directory, where the entries of several departmental or application-specific directories are stored and managed centrally.

Access Management

Access management is the means for controlling user access to enterprise resources. Access management products provide centralized, fine-grained access management for heterogeneous application environments, as well as out-of-the-box integration with Oracle products such as Oracle Portal, Oracle Collaboration Suite, and Oracle E-Business Suite. Oracle access management products include the following:

<u>Oracle Access Manager</u>: Oracle Access Manager provides web-based identity administration, as well as access control to web applications and resources running in heterogeneous environments. It provides the user and group management, delegated administration, password management and self-service functions necessary to manage large user populations in complex, directory-centric environments. Access Manager supports all popular authentication methods including browser forms, digital certificates, and smart cards, and integrates seamlessly with most application servers and portals, including Oracle AS 10g, BEA WebLogic, IBM WebSphere, Vignette and others.

<u>Oracle Identity Federation</u>: Oracle Identity Federation provides a self-contained federation solution that combines the ease of use and portability of a standalone application with a scalable, standards-based proven interoperable architecture.

It helps corporations securely link their business partners into a corporate portal or extranet while also increasing their compliance with privacy and security regulations. Identity Federation enables companies to manage multiple partners and choose from industry standard federated protocols. Identity Federation provides built-in integration with customer's identity management infrastructure (Oracle and non-Oracle) to deliver an end-to-end user experience, addressing scenarios like automatic registration, identity mapping, seamless access control navigation, and others.

<u>Oracle Application Server Single Sign-On</u>: Oracle Application Server Single Sign-On (Oracle AS Single Sign-On) is a component that provides single sign-on access to Oracle and third-party Web applications. Oracle AS Single Sign-On enables Web single sign-on for Oracle applications such as Oracle Portal, Oracle Collaboration Suite and Oracle E-Business Suite.

<u>Oracle Enterprise Single Sign-On Suite</u>: Oracle Enterprise Single Sign-On Suite (eSSO Suite) is a product that provides true single sign-on for all the applications and resources in an enterprise, with no modification required to existing applications. It enables seamless retrofitting of strong, multifactor authentication to the desktop and to all legacy applications.

Identity Management

Oracle Identity Management is a product set that allows enterprises to manage the end-to-end lifecycle of user identities across all enterprise resources both within and beyond the firewall. Oracle identity management products include the following:

<u>Oracle Identity Manager</u>: OIM provides a platform for designing provisioning processes for user and access information to solve the challenge of getting the right accounts and privileges automatically set up for users across all applications they need to access. OIM product framework is architected in a way that allows the developer to choose the level of complexity. Usually, a higher need for customization introduces

higher levels of sophistication in configuration.

<u>Oracle Delegated Administration Services</u>: Oracle Delegated Administration Services, part of Oracle Internet Directory, provides trusted proxy-based administration of directory information by users and application administrators. Oracle Delegated Administration Services are implemented as a set of pre-defined, Web-based units that are embedded in the administrative interfaces for Oracle products such as Oracle AS Portal, Oracle Collaboration Suite, the Oracle Database Security Manager and Oracle E-Business Suite.

Microsoft Solutions

Microsoft Forefront Identity Manager

Microsoft Forefront Identity Manager, provides an integrated and comprehensive solution for managing the entire lifecycle of user identities and their associated credentials. It provides identity synchronization, user provisioning, certificate and password management and policy management in a single solution that works across heterogeneous systems. As a result, IT organizations can define and automate the processes used to manage identities from creation to retirement. It allows you to simplify identity lifecycle management through automated workflows and business rules, and provides easy integration with heterogeneous platforms. Its capabilities includes:

- Policy management
- Credential management
- User management
- Group management
- Access management
- Compliance

Policy management enables:
1. SharePoint-based console for policy authoring, enforcement and auditing
2. Extensible WS-* APIs and Windows Workflow Foundation workflows
3. Heterogeneous identity synchronization and

consistency

Credential management enables:
1. Heterogeneous certificate management with third party CA support
2. Management of multiple credential types
3. Self-service password reset integrated with Windows logon as well as web-based tool
4. Integrated provisioning of identities, credentials, and resources

User management enables:
1. Automated, codeless user provisioning and de-provisioning
2. Self-service user profile management
3. Synchronization of user identity across Active Directory, Microsoft Azure Active Directory and external directories

Group management enables:
1. Rich Office-based self-service group management tools
2. Offline approvals through Office
3. Group and distribution list management including dynamic membership calculation in these groups and DLs based on user's attributes

Access management enables:
1. Preventative role-based access control
2. Rule enforcement through segregation of duties
3. Self-service access request and automated

approval workflow

Compliance enables:
1. Rule-based analytics of access
2. Access re-certification and attestation
3. In-depth reporting and auditing using familiar tools like System Center Service Manager and SQL Server Reporting Services

Bizenit Information Technology Solutions

Smart Identity Self-service

Self-service is the tool that will enable the users of an organization to manage certain services by themselves without any bureaucratic procedures. Self-service helps users to update, manage their personal information, recover the forgotten passwords, manage security token related services, and manage access for temporary visitors.

Self-service can be accessed as a web application which is built on Java, Jscript, and Java script. It is compatible in all browsers like IE, Firefox, and Google Chrome.

Self-Service system contains three modules:

1) Personal information (users can manage their personal information)
2) Password management (users can manage their passwords)
3) Dynamic token management (enables users to provide very strong security with the help of tokens)

The first two data sources are based on the LDAP (Lightweight Directory Access Protocol) server, and the last module's data source is based on the RSA (Remote Secure Access) server.

SIS capabilities include:
- Password reset procedure for end users
- Password policy enforcement
- Self-service portal for updating their personal information
- Support multifactor authentication

Smart Identity Manager

SIM (Smart Identity Manager) is a unique tool fit for LSB (Large Scale Business), MSB (Medium Scale Business), and SSBs (Small Scale Business) for IT account provisioning, administration, reconciliation, password management, governance, analytics, and reporting.

SIM is built on Spring framework, Java, Jquery, and uses LDAP technology supporting databases like Oracle, OpenLDAP, and My SQL. It is compatible and accessible on all web browsers.

SIM contains five modules:
1) User management (manages user information)
2) Group Management (manages users groups, sub-groups, and privileges)
3) Audit (creates and manages reports necessary with audit information)
4) Settings (enables to do configuration on SIM)
5) Statistics (Provides statistical information about the current status of the IT accounts and historical information on the IT accounts)

SIM capabilities include:
- Password reset procedure for end users

340

- Password policy enforcement
- Self-service portal for updating their personal information
- Support multifactor authentication
- Ability to create, update, and delete user accounts in simple approach
- Ability to create, update, and delete groups
- Simplified console management for user account maintenance
- Support for various operating systems
- Integration with Email system
- Integration with LDAP databases
- Integration with other applications like ODSEE
- Integration with other databases like Oracle and MySQL
- Standard reports and configurable reporting

Smart Identity Communicator

SIC (Smart Identity Communicator) is a timely chat tool which enables employees to communicate with each other and helps users seek employees' contact information (like an address book feature provided in MS Exchange server). Using SIC, employees can view the organizational structure and find out others' contact information such as mobile, mail, telephone, facsimile, and so on (MSBs and SSBs who do not want to spend huge amounts of money on MS Exchange server can use this product to save huge amounts of money and attain benefits like communication tool and address book).

SIC allows enterprise employees use a secure mechanism to exchange data without any type of security risks; also, it provides a non-web chat tool and an enterprise address book at the same time.
SIC is a cross-platform application which is developed in Java. It use ODSEE to store user information and is deployed on the tomcat server.

Smart Identity Business Monitoring
SIBM is a server monitoring system used for monitoring identity management applications, databases, and tools. SIBM uses different active and passive polling methods for identifying problems and issues in smart identity product suite.
It is a standard J2EE program which supports monitoring target objects without performing any code changes to the customer's products.
SIBM capabilities include:

- Visual display of IDM architecture health status
- Strong scalability options
- Supports flexible scheduling task execution cycle
- Convenient alarm and notification strategy configuration
- Alarm or system recovery notification emails
- Statistical analysis based on monitoring and alarm data

Smart Identity Reverse Agent

SIRA (Smart Identity Reverse Agent) is a high performance reverse proxy server. It supports deployments in a variety of application servers. This is a unique product which provides many functions like automatic structure login form, cookie management, header management, etc.

SIRA is a standard J2EE program which can be used for searching, transitioning, and dealing with HTTP requests sent to the target systems (All of these functions do not need any modifications to the target applications).

SIRA capabilities include:

- Reverse proxy and helping target systems hide IP and other sensitive information to protect the front end.

- Cookie management, managing, and reposting cookies.

- Capture request, supporting capture requests, and store them in local files which can be used for auditing.

- Header management, managing the addition and removal of header, and setting values in header.

- Extract entity, searching entities from HTTP requests, and getting values and assigning them specific variables.

- Static request management, managing GET and POST requests, and setting static values directly.
- File processing to find attributes in a file and assign them to specific variables.

Acronyms

ABAC – Attribute Based Access Control
ACC – Availability, Capacity and Continuity
AD – Active Directory
ADDS – Active Directory Domain Services
ADFS – Active Directory Federation Services
AFC –Active Failover Cluster
ALM – Application Lifecycle Management
APS – Application Protection System
BCM – Business Continuity Management
BCP – Business Continuity Planning
BYOD – Bring Your Own Device
BYOI – Bring Your Own Identity
CA – Certificate Authority
CAC – Cyber Access Control
CER – Crossover Error Rate
CFC – Cold failover cluster
COBIT – Control Objectives for Information Technology
CSF – Critical Success Factors
DAC – Discretionary Access Control
DAML – Directory Access Markup Language
DAP – Directory Access Protocol
DC – Domain Controllers
DEN – Directory Enabled Network
DIT – Directory Information Tree
DLP – Data Loss/Leakage Prevention
DN – Distinguished Name
DNS – Domain Name System

DOS – Denial of Service
DRM – Digital Rights Management
DSML – Directory Services Markup Language
ELS – Early Life Support
ESSO – Enterprise Single Sign On
EUA – Enterprise User Administration
EVMS – Enterprise Vulnerability Management System
FAR – False Acceptance Rate
FRR – False Rejection Rate
GLBA – Gramm-Leach-Bliley Act
GRC – Governance, Risk and Compliance
GRCM – Governance, Risk and Compliance Management
GUID – Global Unique Identifier
HIPAA – Health Insurance Portability and Accountability Act
HTTP – Hypertext transfer protocol
IAAS – Infrastructure as a service
IAG– Identity and Access Governance
IAI – Identity and Access Intelligence
IAM – Identity and Access Management
IAMS –Identity and Access Management Service
IAP – Identity Assertion Provider
IDaaS – Identity as a service
IdP– Identity Provider
IFH – Identity Federation Hub
IGF – Identity Governance Framework
IS – Information Security
ISO/IEC – International Organization for Standardization/International Electrotechnical Commission

ITIL – Information Technology Infrastructure Library
ITSCM - Information Technology Service Continuity Management
KB – Knowledge base
KBA – Knowledge Based Authentication
LA – Lead Auditor
LI – Lead Implementer
LDAP – Lightweight Directory Access Protocol
LDIF – LDAP Directory Interchange Format
MAC – Mandatory Access Control
MIAM – Mobile Identity and Access Management
MOF – Microsoft Operations Framework
OAM – Oracle Access Manager
OIM – Oracle Identity Manager
OLA – Operational Level Agreements
ORT – Operational Readiness Testing
OTP – One Time Password
OU – Organizational Unit
PAAM – Privileged Account Access management
PAAS – Platform as a service
PBAC – Policy Based Access Control
PDP – Policy Decision Point
PEP – Policy Enforcement Point
PIM – Privileged Identity Management
PIN – Personal Identification Number
PKI – Public Key Infrastructure
PKE – Public Key Enablement
POC – Proof of Concept
RBAC – Role Based Access Control
RBAC – Risk Based Access Control
REST – Representational State Transfer

SAAS – Software as a service
SAML – Security Assertion Markup Language
SCIM – Simple Cloud Identity Management
SIBM – Smart Identity Business Monitoring
SIEM – Security Information and Event Management
SIC – Smart Identity Communicator
SIM – Smart Identity Manager
SLA – Service Level Agreement
SP – Service Provider
SPML – Security Provisioning Markup Language
SPOC – Single Point of Contact
STS – Security Token Service
SOAP – Simple Object Access Protocol
SOD – Segregation of Duties
SOP – Standard Operating Procedures
SOX – Sarbanes Oxley Act
SSH – Secure Shell
SSL – Secure Socket Layer
SSO – Single Sign On
ESSO – Enterprise Single Sign On
TCO – Total cost of ownership
TOGAF – The Open Group Architecture Framework
UC – Underpinning Contracts
UI – User Interface
WSS – Web services security
XKMS – XML Key Management Services
XML – Extensible Markup Language
XACML – Extensible Access Control Markup Language

Index

351